Learn to
Relax

THIRD EDITION

Proven Techniques for Reducing Stress, Tension,
and Anxiety—and Promoting Peak Performance

C. Eugene Walker

John Wiley & Sons, Inc.

NEW YORK · CHICHESTER · WEINHEIM · BRISBANE · SINGAPORE · TORONTO

This book is affectionately dedicated to my sister, Rita, who taught me much about the art of living and to her children, James Todd and Lisa Gene, who help to make life richly rewarding.

Library of Congress Cataloging-in-Publication Data:

Walker, C. Eugene (Clarence Eugene), 1939-

    Learn to relax : proven techniques for reducing stress, tension, and anxiety—and promoting peak performance / C. Eugene Walker.—3rd ed.

      p. cm.

    Includes index.

    ISBN 0-471-37776-7 (pbk. : alk. paper)

    1. Anxiety.   2. Relaxation.   3. Conduct of life.   I. Title.

    BF575.A6 W34 2001

    155.9'042—dc21   00-036495

Printed in the United States of America.

10 9 8 7 6 5 4 3 2 1

Contents

Preface

A basic fact of life is that each individual experiences stress, tension, and anxiety as a part of his or her existence. Sometimes the experience is mild and passes quickly; sometimes it is agonizingly severe and may last for long periods of time. Although humans have always experienced these feelings, some think that the nature of current civilization and technology may be causing our tensions and anxieties to escalate at a rate faster than that of our ability to cope with them. It is impossible to know whether this is true. The basic fact that these experiences are a part of living, however, remains with us. Psychologists have developed numerous ways to treat anxiety and related problems in those who come to them for help. In this book you will find specific techniques, many of them fairly new, explained in such a way that you can use them yourself. These techniques have helped many people; it is my hope that they will be useful to you.

The first and second editions of this book proved to be helpful to thousands of people. These editions consisted of text only, containing information I'd found helpful in my work as a psychotherapist. Over the years, as a result of the publication of those editions, I was frequently asked to speak on stress management to various groups. From these experiences I developed a workshop on stress management and, later, a graduate course on stress. The basic principles of psychology outlined in this book work equally well for the treatment of clinical problems and for coping with everyday situational problems. When presenting these concepts in a workshop or course, I found it helpful for the participants to use practical exercises to understand the concepts better and to help apply them to their own lives. Thus, in this edition, I have included exercises after each chapter that will facilitate understanding and application. It is hoped that this will make the book more suitable for use in workshops and as a supplementary text in courses, as well as making it more profitable for personal study.

Throughout the book the reader will find references to other books and articles. If such a source is quoted in the present work, I have included full reference information. If the book is mentioned only in passing, as something one might read for additional information, only the author and title are presented. The reader should have no trouble finding any of the materials mentioned in the present text at a local bookstore, from new or used book sites on the Internet (e.g., at Amazon.com, BarnesandNoble.com, Bookfinder.com), or at a library if they are out of print. At the end of the present book you will find a selected list of particularly helpful books for further reading that were in print in inexpensive editions at the time this manuscript went to press.

I

What Is Anxiety?

BECAUSE ANXIETY IS such a simple word and common experience for all people, it may come as a surprise that psychologists do not really know exactly what it is. In fact, some psychologists have argued that the term itself is so vague and so general that it is useless for precise communication. While this may seem like nonsense (psychology is sometimes called "the science of making common sense unintelligible") there are problems in clearly defining what we mean by *anxiety*.

The reason is that the word is used to cover a large number of situations. For example, you may say to me that you are anxious; this may be a *subjective feeling* that you are reporting. I may have guessed you were feeling that way, depending on your outward behavior. If I ask further, I may find that your mind seems to be racing and is full of worries, fears, and ideas that keep recurring. You may also experience various physical sensations, but they may not seem to be especially prominent; the anxiety seems to be centered in your head.

A closely related situation that we would also label *anxiety* is *mental blocking*. For example, if you are very tense about an exam, you may study diligently and know the material thoroughly before

There are problems in clearly defining what we mean by anxiety.

I

the test. When the test is presented, however, you may find, to your consternation, that your mind is blank; nothing that was studied can be remembered. As soon as the exam hour is over, however, the memory magically returns. An understanding instructor may allow you to complete the exam, even though the time is up. One way of coping with the mental block is to quit trying for a while. You might get a drink of water, take a short walk, sharpen a pencil, or do something of that sort. Often a person in such a situation is trying too hard. Breaking the mental set lets you get a fresh start and get over the blocking.

On other occasions, you might say that your mind or head is clear, but that you are experiencing *physical sensations* or problems that you call anxiety. These sensations may include one or more of the following, as well as a host of others: muscular tightness, nausea, stiff neck, general or localized body pain, respiratory problems, rapid or irregular heartbeat, dry mouth, hot flashes, chills, sweating (especially on the hands), excessive urination, diarrhea, loss of appetite, and sleep disturbances.

On the other hand, you might deny subjective feelings of anxiety or worry, have no mental blocking, and also claim that none of the physical symptoms just mentioned are present. I might still find that you are anxious, however, if I note such *behaviors* as changes in normal speech patterns, stuttering, stammering, distinctive facial expressions, tics or twitches, physical awkwardness, making mental errors, or having accidents. When I was a graduate student of psychology at Purdue University, my peers and I lived under a great deal of tension and anxiety about our studies and our futures. All graduate students feel such pressure. A standing joke with us was to walk up to a fellow student and ask if he was anxious. The correct response to this question was to give an exaggerated startle response, then purse the lips and calmly say, "Nope."

If you have one or any combination of the previous signs, you might say that you are anxious, or others might consider you to be anxious. To complicate matters further, at different times in your life, perhaps in response to different situations, you might show different patterns of these signs. We would label them all anxiety.

To complicate matters still further, studies of all these components indicate that different people experience different patterns and combinations of the above in the same situation. They would all say, however, that they were anxious. So the word does cover a multitude of experiences, some of which are subjective feelings; some, mental reactions; some, physical reactions; and some, changes in behavior.

Anxiety seems to be everywhere and in everyone. Excessive anxiety is considered to be one of the major symptoms of emotional disturbance, and some have speculated that the nature of humans may be to be chronically, mildly disturbed, at least in civilized society as we know it today. Some biologists and anthropologists argue that this is the case because in our evolutionary history, the survival of the beast known as homo sapiens depended on a combination of physical aggressiveness and mental foresight. This beast, however, now finds itself in a society that permits its powers of foresight to run wild (even feeds and exaggerates them with communications media) but forbids the use of physical force or aggression to solve problems.

Anxiety is the reaction we have to a situation in which we believe our well-being is endangered or threatened in some way.

The famous physiologist Walter B. Cannon demonstrated that the nervous system of humans prepares them physically for fight or flight in the face of danger. Today, unfortunately, neither of these options is very effective. If we are physically aggressive, we are likely to be arrested. If we attempt to flee our obligations, we will be located and returned to the situation. Thus, homo sapiens may be like cornered animals that experience a chronic state of anxiety and fear in a complex world. In the later chapters of this book, however, we will see that such a pessimistic prospect is not inevitable.

Because *anxiety* is such a vague term, it might be helpful to define the several related terms that describe human experience in this area. Psychologists differ in their use of these terms depending on their ideas about personality and psychotherapy; the following definitions are simple ones that will serve for our discussion.

While there is no completely adequate definition of *anxiety*, we might refer to it as the reaction we have to a situation in which we believe our well-being is endangered or threatened in some way. This may be any form of well-being. We may feel that our physical safety is in danger, or our success in our job, or our self-esteem, or the well-being of someone important to us, as in the case of the parent anxiously waiting for a child to return from a date. Saying you are nervous is pretty much synonymous with saying you are anxious.

Tension may be thought of as chronic, usually low-level anxiety that is experienced as a part of an ongoing situation in which we are involved.

Fear is intense anxiety experienced in response to a specific threat. A *phobia* is an intense, incapacitating, and irrational fear attached to a specific thing or situation. Most people have some phobias, whether they are of blood, bugs, snakes, airplanes, or whatever. We used to give impressive Greek names to each phobia: claustrophobia (fear of enclosed places), acrophobia (fear of high places), hydrophobia (fear of water), and so forth. Today clinicians simply label the problem a *phobia* and plainly state what the object of fear is. Chapter 6 presents a technique that eliminates phobias in a relatively short period of time.

The term *unconscious anxiety* may mean many things, but basically, as we might expect, it is anxiety of which we are not consciously aware. For example, often we don't realize how tense or anxious we were about a matter until it has passed. The relief we feel at that moment makes us reflect on the past and decide that we were anxious at the time. Yet, we did not consciously label the sensation as such at the time it was occurring.

Free-floating anxiety describes a situation in which intense anxiety seems unexpectedly to attack a person, only to go away, then return later. Generally one realizes that he or she is under a great deal of general tension or strain but is unable to connect specific events with the attacks.

Tension *is chronic, usually low-level anxiety that is experienced as a part of an ongoing situation in which we are involved.*

Fear *is intense anxiety experienced in response to a specific threat.*

A phobia *is an intense, incapacitating, and irrational fear attached to a specific thing or situation.*

Panic is a condition in which the anxiety has become so great that the individual loses control of the situation. The person often becomes confused and may do bizarre things. It is a very painful and unpleasant experience. Many emotionally disturbed people seem to live in a chronic state of panic or near panic; when we deal with them, it helps to keep in mind the intense anxiety they are experiencing. Gentleness, patience, and help in structuring things so the emotionally troubled can handle them go a long way with such people.

Stress is a term that has come to be used almost synonymously with *anxiety*, but it includes some extra and important dimensions. In the physical sciences, stress is the effect of placing a load on an object, such as weight on a bridge. Obviously the bridge can hold only so much weight before it breaks. Other factors such as wind and temperature may also impinge on the bridge's ability to hold. In psychology we often use the term *stress* to describe the amount of pressure from the environment that one can handle before beginning to develop problems in coping. Thus, Richard Lazarus, one of the foremost authorities on stress, offers the following definition: "Psychological stress is a particular relationship between the person and the environment that is appraised by the person as taxing or exceeding his or her resources and endangering his or her well-being" (Richard S. Lazarus and Susan Folkman, *Stress, Appraisal, and Coping.* New York: Springer Publishing Co., 1984, p. 19).

An expanded view of the concept of emotional stress is possible if we consider the term's origin in science and engineering. We can then understand that some stress is good. For example, a structure that was designed to bear weight is actually more stable when the stress of an appropriate weight is placed on it. This is sometimes referred to as *eustress* (positive stress). However, when the stress exceeds the capacity to handle it, we have what may be called *distress* (negative stress). Sometimes stress is neither helpful nor harmful; this is referred to as *neustress* (neutral stress). A complete definition of stress emphasizes the interaction among the

Unconscious anxiety *is anxiety of which we are not consciously aware.*

Free-floating anxiety *describes a situation in which intense anxiety seems unexpectedly to attack a person, only to go away, then return later.*

Panic *is a condition in which the anxiety has become so great that the individual loses control of the situation.*

load from the environment; the resiliency of the individual; and the wide variety of other factors, such as the pattern of stress (the fact that the same stressors that may be handled with ease if distributed over time can become overwhelming if they cluster and are experienced all at once). The interaction among these factors may influence the effect stress has (positive, negative, or neutral).

One of the pioneers in the area of stress research was Hans Selye, who identified three stages of reaction to a stressor. The first is alarm and mobilization, in which the body begins to battle the stressor. The second is resistance, in which the body attempts to withstand the pressure. This is followed by exhaustion and disintegration, in which the body breaks down and physical symptoms occur such as high blood pressure, headaches, infections, and so forth. Selye called this the *general adaptation syndrome* and felt that it explained the appearance of psychosomatic diseases as well as our sometimes increased susceptibility to organic illness. In extreme or prolonged cases, the result is death. From this it might seem that stress is the great enemy of human beings. This is only partly true, however. Stress and anxiety are a lot like pain: We prefer to experience as little of them as possible, but they serve a very useful purpose in alerting us and activating our defenses in times of danger. Moderate amounts of stress or anxiety motivate us to plan for future events and increase our ability (primarily through the secretion of adrenalin) to cope with situations as they occur. The increased strength of a person who is afraid, or the ability of some individuals to work better under a little pressure, are examples of the beneficial nature of stress.

I recall that, when preparing for the major comprehensive exams that would determine whether I would receive my degree in psychology, I became much more mentally alert than usual. I found myself able to read more quickly than normal, and I developed an almost photographic memory for what I'd read (which was unusual for me). I was experiencing more stress than I might have otherwise because the exams took place in January, which is preceded by football bowl games. Since I regard football as an art form, I had not spent enough time studying for the exams. Fortunately, rather than causing a mental block, the stress heightened my capacity to function academically.

Moderate anxiety also serves to protect us from danger. A study done some years ago identified three types of guppies with respect to their reactions to the sight of smallmouth bass, which feed on guppies, in an adjacent tank. One group were timid. They swam away and hid when they saw the bass. Ordinary guppies swam away but did not make extra efforts to hide. Bold guppies held their ground and did not avoid the bass. Later, groups of the three types of guppies were put in a tank with the bass. After 60 hours, 40% of the timid guppies were still alive. However, only 15% of the ordinary guppies survived and none of the bold ones.

It is when stress or anxiety become excessive and/or prolonged that they become a problem. Those who have studied human activation have noted that this is a common feature of many motivating forces. When they are present in moderate amounts, increasing those amounts leads to heightened performance. Eventually, however, a peak is reached after which any additional amount results in deterioration of the performance. This is certainly the case with anxiety: A little brings out the best in us. A life without emotion, stress and anxiety included, would be very drab. Yet, too much is debilitating. This is part of the fascination of amusement parks. We can administer small amounts of anxiety to ourselves in controlled conditions and feel the joy of its immediate dissipation. Likewise, thriller books and movies are fun because they excite and activate us with an exhilarating feeling in a situation that we know is really quite safe. The person who enjoys challenges does the same thing in real life. We would not enjoy amusement parks, however, if our lives were actually in danger on the rides. Nor would we welcome challenges or tasks in our lives that we were not able to cope with. Such situations would be destructive and debilitating rather than pleasurable.

Excessive anxiety inhibits and defeats us. We have all been frozen by fear or have been unable to perform simple functions in front of an audience that made us nervous. I recall an example of this effect of anxiety from my undergraduate days. I was taking a course in French, and each day we were assigned translations to do at night that we were to recite the next day in class. I used to labor over these translations for hours each night, looking up every word and puzzling over the syntax to make the translation as close to perfect as possible. It was always embarrassing to make a mistake in front of the whole class.

One day I failed to do the translation ahead of time and had decided to cut class. On the way across campus I ran into my French instructor. I explained to him that I had not had time to do the translation for the day and that I did not want to take his time without being prepared. He suggested that I come along anyway and just listen. When it was my turn to recite, however, he asked if I would like to try it even though I wasn't prepared. I decided I would, and found to my surprise that I was able to read the lesson without hesitation as though it were in English. I stopped only at words in the new vocabulary for the day and easily went on after they were supplied by the instructor. The fact was that by removing all pressure to perform and anxiety about perfection, I was able to perform better than ever. I felt no pressure because, after all, I hadn't prepared and couldn't be expected to do very well. I had never been able to do that before and have never been able to do it since.

In the chapters to follow we will learn a number of specific ways to keep stress and anxiety in check so that they enhance rather than inhibit performance. Stress and anxiety are facts of existence. It is best to learn to make them work for us rather than against us. There is an old military saying: "Don't sweat the small stuff." One might add, "Everything is small stuff." When confronted with a threat, our bodies prepare us for fight or flight; but if you can't fight or flee, flow.

STRESS MANAGEMENT EXERCISES

Having read the material in the preceding section, answer the following questions.

1. Several terms regarding tension, stress, and anxiety were defined. Which one of these terms describes your most common experience in this area?

_____

_____

2. Are there any that you have never experienced (e.g., free-floating anxiety, blocking, etc.)? Which one(s)?

_____

_____

_____

_____

_____

3. In what area do you usually experience stress or anxiety the most (mental, physical, behavioral)?

_____

_____

_____

4. What have you found from experience that helps control stress or anxiety in this area? What makes it worse?

_____

_____

_____

_____

_____

_____

_____

_____

5. Think of the time in your life when you were the most worried, anxious, or stressed that you can recall. Write a description of that situation in the following space, including: (a) what was going on; (b) how you felt; (c) how the situation came out; and (d) what you can learn from the situation as you look back on it.

_____

_____

_____

_____

_____

_____

_____

_____

_____

_____

_____

_____

_____

_____

6. In most cases the things we worry about never happen; or if they do, they are not nearly as bad as we thought they would be. Was this true for you in the example in Item 5? What can you learn from that?

_____

_____

_____

_____

_____

_____

_____

_____

_____

7. Think of a time when stress improved your performance. Write a description of that situation, including: (a) what was going on; (b) how you felt; (c) how the situation came out; and (d) what you can learn from this situation as you look back on it.

_____

_____

_____

_____

_____

_____

_____

_____

_____

_____

_____

_____

_____

_____

8. How can you use the lessons learned from the exercise in Item 7 to improve your performance in everyday life?

_____

_____

_____

_____

9. As discussed in this chapter, there are many positive aspects to stress, anxiety and related experiences. List some of the positives from your point of view.

_____

_____

_____

_____

_____

_____

_____

_____

_____

_____

_____

_____

_____

_____

10. Ask a friend to answer these same questions, then share your reactions with each other.

_____

_____

_____

_____

_____

_____

_____

_____

2

Straight Thinking

MANY ANXIETIES ARISE from thoughts we have or interpretations of events in our lives that we know, intellectually, should not be anything to worry about. We tell ourselves that a certain situation is not very important, that there are many ways to look at it, and that it shouldn't bother us. And yet, it does bother us. It can haunt and nag us daily, causing anxiety, irritability, and misery. Friends reassure us, and we tell them we know that what they are saying is true but we still can't get our worries out of our heads. Sometimes, in cases like this the main problem is faulty thinking. If we can think clearly and straighten things out in our minds, the problem dissolves.

One psychologist, Dr. Albert Ellis, has studied this aspect of anxiety for many years. He has developed a system of counseling and psychotherapy based on the idea of straight thinking. He calls his treatment rational-emotive behavior therapy. Often, to make the technique of his therapy clear, he refers to the *ABC's of emotional problems* in the following manner. Generally when an Activating event (*A*) occurs, it seems to cause an emotional reaction or Consequence (*C*) in a person. On closer examination, however, we find that *A* did not, in fact, cause *C*. What caused *C* was the Belief system (*B*) of the person. Thus, we have the ABC's of anxiety.

We will get to *D* when we talk about the remedy for this situation; but first, let's look at a couple of examples of how these ABC's can happen in everyday life. Suppose a person makes a mistake at work. That is *A*—the fact of what happened. Often *A* activates a Belief system (*B*) that runs something like this: "I did a bad job today. Isn't that horrible? I always do that. I'm really incompetent at everything I do. I'll never succeed. I'm terrible. Most people know that about me. Nobody really respects me. I'll never be accepted or have any close friends at work because they know how bad I am." The emotional consequence, *C*, of course, is anxiety, depression, and loss of self-esteem. However, as Ellis would point out to such a person, this is *catastrophizing*. The individual is overreacting to the facts of the situation, and because of his or her faulty belief system, he or she actually produces the catastrophic consequence. This is irrational. If the individual could be rational about it, he or she wouldn't feel that badly at all.

Let's look at another example: Suppose a normal, average, likable teenage boy asks a girl for a date and she turns him down. This might activate a belief system that says the following: "She doesn't like me well enough to go out with me even once. I must not be much of a man. All girls probably feel that way about me. This is awful. I'm a lousy excuse for a person. I'll never find the right girl to marry." The result, again, is anxiety, depression, and rumination about "Who am I? Why am I so worthless?" This is a common reaction among young adults and sometimes older ones, too. If that were all that happened, it would be bad enough; but it usually gets worse. The person left anxious and depressed by this small event in life often finds that the reaction to this event becomes, in turn, an activating event for other false belief systems, which then cause additional emotional consequences. The individual continues in this way to dig a deeper and deeper hole, which he or she will never get out of if something doesn't happen to stop the process. Eventually this kind of process results in the individual's preoccupation and distraction from meeting major responsibilities in life. He or she becomes tired and inefficient.

There is a solution, however. A person doesn't have to be victimized by these irrational belief systems. The answer is in learning to Dispute (D) them successfully. This calls for clear, rational thinking. Let's go back to the person who made a mistake at work that day. He or she could say something like this to herself: "I made a mistake today. Well, you win some and you lose some. Everybody has some good days and some bad days. I guess I am just part of the human race. But, the important thing in life is to *learn* from failure. Everybody fails and does a bad job sometimes. Nobody is exempt from that. The really successful people are the ones who learn from their mistakes and go back to do a better job the next time. Let me see . . . What can I learn from today? How can I do better tomorrow?" After some thought, he or she might add, "I feel better now. I know what I can do to continue to get better at my job all the time."

The important thing in life is to learn *from failure*

The teenager who was turned down for the date might say to himself, "She doesn't want to date me now. Maybe she will some other time. There could be a lot of reasons for her to say no that have nothing to do with me. Even if she doesn't like me at all, there are many other girls I can date. All guys—even movie stars—are turned down by someone in their lives. It's really a minor thing. Someday I'll meet the right girl and we'll get along fine."

The points made in this chapter involve *mental processes*. They are intended to combat irrational belief systems that cause anxiety—and a great deal of anxiety is caused by just such beliefs. *Behavior* is part of it, too; along with thinking clearly, we need to be doing the right things and improving our actual performance all the time.

Many people find information to dispute irrational belief systems by reading autobiographies of well-known people. It often helps eliminate irrational beliefs to learn that others, even very successful and famous people, have had the same experiences and feelings that we have had. For example, Louis Pasteur failed the admission exams for the University of Paris and wasn't admitted

Remember: All people have the occasional setback. Such an event can be a stimulus for growth and improvement if we see it as such, rather than allowing it to provoke the anxiety that leads to deterioration.

on his first try. Even after he got in, he was regarded as a rather mediocre student and as somewhat of a plodder by his professors. Albert Einstein once failed an elementary math course. Thomas Edison was expelled from school as uneducable. Dwight Eisenhower was a constant discipline problem at West Point and was almost expelled on more than one occasion. Johnny Unitas was cut from the Baltimore Colts the first time he tried out. One could go on, with an endless list of authors who received hundreds of rejection slips before ever being published, artists who weren't recognized until after they had died, and so forth. The important thing to remember is that all people have setbacks. These events needn't have catastrophic consequences if we think rationally about what has occurred and what it means. Such an event can be a stimulus for growth and improvement if we see it as such, rather than allowing it to provoke the anxiety that leads to deterioration.

In analyzing Western culture, Ellis and others have identified prevalent myths and ideas that are irrational leading to problems in our thinking which result in negative emotional reactions.

1. *We must be loved by everyone, and everyone must approve of everything we do.* This idea leads to much irrational concern, especially when there are signs that somebody, anybody, doesn't like us or disapproves of something we are doing. It is a useless position to take because it is not possible for everyone to like us. Nobody can please everybody. The very things that make one liked and approved of by one person make him or her despised by another. To try to be loved by everyone only makes a person less self-directing, more insecure, and less interesting. It is desirable to be loved, and it's necessary to be sensitive to feedback from others in order to relate to them more effectively; but you shouldn't try to be loved by everyone. Rather, you should actively seek out other people with similar interests and values so that you'll get along well with them. It's better to spend our energy selecting and cultivating real friends than to try to please everybody and anybody.

In counseling young people, I frequently find that while they are in the public school system, they want to be popular with everyone at school. This creates a very great problem. The range of interests, socioeconomic levels, family backgrounds, and so on in a school population are so great that receiving universal approval is impossible. Yet they're thrown in with this large group every day, and they want to be approved of by them. The problem frequently diminishes after graduation because they can selectively associate with people of tastes and values similar to their own. In general, it's best to maintain our own sense of personal integrity, being true to our own values while striving to be loving, creative, productive, and contributing individuals. If we do that, we can let people like us or not as they choose and not be overly anxious about it. We'll have more real friends and be less plagued by irrational anxiety if we do.

To try to be loved by everyone only makes a person less self-directing, more insecure, and less interesting. It's better to spend our energy selecting and cultivating real friends than to try to please everybody and anybody.

2 . *We must be thoroughly competent, adequate, intelligent, and achieving in everything we do.* It is obviously not possible to do everything well; it's even impossible to be truly perfect at any one thing. A person who adopts such standards is constantly full of anxiety about past failures to achieve perfection and the possibility that he or she will fail to achieve perfection in the future. Even one who is acknowledged by others to be the best in an area today (note that this is not the same as being *perfect*) is continually anxious about falling from this position tomorrow. He or she may begin to decline, or a new and better challenger may appear. People with this irrational fear of failure often achieve a lot, especially in the short run, but they generally don't enjoy it. Often the methods they use to achieve success alienate others. In the long run, many such people do not really achieve full potential because of faulty belief systems.

It is best to realize that we are not, and will not be, deities. We can't be more than human. Nobody, including ourselves, should expect that of us. We should strive for achievement

It is obviously not possible to do everything well. Nobody, including ourselves, should expect that of us. We should strive for achievement and accomplishment, but we should do so in the sense of making progress, learning, and growing as we live.

and accomplishment, but we should do so in the sense of making progress, learning, and growing as we live. We must recognize all the time that as humans we will make mistakes; we will fail; we will have faults; and we will be subject to limitations and frailties. We won't be perfect, but we will do what we can and will improve as we go along. That is all anybody has a right to ask of us.

3. *Many people around us are wicked, evil, deliberately do us harm and should be severely punished.* There are few absolute rights or wrongs. There are things other people do that we wouldn't do; things they do that we consider inappropriate or antisocial; and things we simply wish they wouldn't do. Yet these people are not necessarily bad people. Blaming them does no good. Punishing them does little, if any, good and often does harm. If we analyze why they did something, we can almost always see the sense of it from their point of view. Thus, their actions could be expected. If they were wrong (at least as we view things) in what they did, it's generally due to stupidity, ignorance, or emotional disturbance; so we should be tolerant of their behavior and try to educate, redirect, and help them change to more desirable behavior. If we do so, we all come out ahead in the end.

Likewise, we should give ourselves the same break. If someone doesn't like what we've done, we should not become anxious or upset about it. We should recognize that, from where they stand, our behavior seemed inappropriate; we should not be blamed for that. Nor should we become anxious and depressed about it. The rational thing to do is to compare ideas, discuss them, and see if we can learn from the experience. One or both of us may change, or we may agree to disagree; either way is better than engaging in blaming and mutual hostility over a period of time, which leaves us both losers.

4. *It is a terrible catastrophe when things are not as we would like them to be; the world should be fair and just.* This notion is obviously

silly and childish when we think about it clearly, but many times we do proceed with the assumption that the world and everything in it should be just the way we want it to be. We are deeply offended and outraged when we see signs to the contrary. With all the different kinds of people in the world, however, it could not possibly be to everyone's liking. The harsh reality of the universe is that it was not created only for our pleasure, to revolve around us personally. Nor, as my mother told me, is it always fair.

Therefore we have to accept that the world, even our corner of it, will never be exactly the way we would like it. We should not expect it to be. When we see something we don't like, it does no good to perceive it as a personal insult or as an attempt to defeat us. What we should do is say, "That is too bad," or, "I don't like that," and then try to do something constructive to change or improve it. As someone has said, if you are unavoidably dealt a lemon in life, you may as well make some lemonade. On the other hand, if the situation can't be improved at all, then we should resign ourselves to accepting it, realizing that this is sometimes the nature of things. We often tell our children that they have to realize that they can't have everything they want. Sometimes, though, as adults we make the same error in more subtle, sophisticated ways. When we do, it can lead only to unnecessary upset and anxiety. I am reminded of the definition of a *pesoptimist:* a person who thinks that the best possible thing will happen to him or her, but that it won't be good enough.

5. *Unhappiness is the result of external events and happenings that are forced on us and that we have no control over.* Actually, 99% of the unhappiness we experience is not caused by the unpleasant aspects of real life events but is *created internally,* by the things we say to ourselves about those events. We can control the external events to only a certain extent, but we can learn to control our internal responses to these events almost completely. For example, if I lose my wallet with $1,000 in it, I

may become very anxious, depressed, and unhappy about it. The actual event, however, is not that bad. It will take me maybe an hour to notify credit card companies and the various governmental agencies. I will have to buy a new wallet, and I lost $1,000. Viewed in terms of a lifetime, the loss of the money and time are, in fact, very small; but by overreacting, I make the event worse and exaggerate its significance.

We actually defeat ourselves with our internal reactions. The external event, if viewed rationally, would be a matter of only minor concern. We can often see the truth of this when someone else is involved, thinking, "I wish I had *his* problems," or "I wish that were *my* main problem." We also need to see the truth of it in our own experience.

6. *We should be greatly concerned about dangerous and fearful things and must center our thinking on them until the danger has passed.* This is an irrational idea because such thinking will not prevent the things from happening. In some cases, it even makes them more likely to happen. In other cases, we become so exhausted from worrying that when the bad thing does happen we are less able to cope than if we had not worried so much. Also, the large majority of things about which we worry never occur, and if they do, they are not as bad as we had expected. The best thing to do is face such situations head-on. We should strive to make them nondangerous and to handle them successfully when they do happen, but excessive worrying about them serves no purpose. Even if the worst occurs, we should regard it realistically as an unpleasant event, one that we didn't like, and go on from there. We need to stop telling ourselves that every problem is a terrible thing and that it is the precursor to the end of the world. It is not. The fact is that we can deal with anything that comes our way and go on with our life no matter what it is—with the right attitude. Successful people do what they have to do, and 99% of what they have to do concerns their attitudes.

7. *It's easier to avoid difficulties and responsibilities in life than it is to face them.* When we try to avoid difficulties and responsibilities, we only create more and worse problems in the future. It is best to face problems squarely and to solve them to the best of our abilities. Putting them off only increases anxiety, depression, and guilt. Facing them increases our feelings of self-confidence, self-esteem, and happiness. The enjoyable life is not one without problems; it is one in which we solve problems successfully.

The enjoyable life is not one without problems; it is one in which we solve problems successfully.

8. *We need someone or something stronger than ourselves to rely on.* Nobody is completely independent, and we should have no fear of being dependent on others to some extent, as they are on us. We should realize, however, that this dependency is a matter of every human being's need for others. It is not so specific that we must have one certain person on which to depend. If one person fails us or is unavailable, there are other people who can help. One person's whole life is never dependent on a single other person. Sometimes we may think it is, but it isn't. Life goes on with or without any one individual. On the other side of the coin, we need to develop our own integrity, independence, individuality, and self-expression so that the failure or loss of someone close to us is not devastating. Being overly dependent on another robs both us and them of the best in life. We become insecure and fail to learn and to grow. They, in turn, are burdened with us and cannot reach their full potential.

Being overly dependent on another robs both us and them of the best in life.

A part of this dependency is often expressed as a feeling that people owe us things because we did something for them once or that we are obligated to them for something they did. Neither of these is true. If we want to do something for someone, we should do it, and there should be no strings attached. We should expect nothing in return except the gratification that we did what we thought was right and what we wanted to do. Likewise, we should not feel obligated to others under similar circumstances. It is irrational and pointless to suffer anguish because somebody returns nothing, or even ill, for our kindnesses. This does not preclude, of course, striking a clear bargain in which the terms are stipulated and understood by each party at the time. We do give to get on occasion. But we also should give a lot just because we want to give, expecting nothing in return. If we do, we'll get our share, in the long run. It is of no profit to keep score and worry if we seem to be a point or two behind.

9. *Because something greatly influenced us in the past, it must determine our present behavior; the influence of the past cannot be overcome.* This is not true at all. While it is often difficult to change previous learnings, it is not impossible. The essence of life is growth and development. We never stop changing. We are not the same people we were 10 years ago; nor are the world and our circumstances the same. We need to learn from past experiences but not be overly attached to them. What may have been necessary and appropriate in the past may not fit or work at all in the present. The rational person develops and improves throughout life. Even things that are inherited are almost always capable of being influenced by our behavior; we are not victims of our genes. We may have inherited a temperament that makes us easily irritable, but we can learn to control anger. We may have a tendency to put on weight easily, but proper diet and exercise can prevent obesity.

10. *What other people do is vitally important to us, and we should make every effort to change them to be the way we think they should be.* Actually, other people's lives, problems, and behaviors are their own business and generally no concern of ours. We cannot control or change them very much. Efforts to do so backfire more often than not and serve only to worsen the situation. In general, we should strive for the utmost tolerance, to live and let live.

Often we are more upset by the implications or interpretations we think are involved in their behavior than by the

The essence of life is growth and development. We're always changing. We are not victims of our genes.

behavior itself. Usually the supposed implications and interpretations are not in the other person's mind at all. If the other person asks for help in changing his or her behavior and we want to give assistance, we may. Yet we have no reason to force our help on those who don't want it. If their behavior directly affects us, we may want to discuss it with them and seek a solution. Many times, however, we may just have to learn to live with the situation. A professor of psychology in my freshman year at college used to repeat in his lectures, "We may as well learn that people have faults and decide to live with them anyhow."

11. *There is one perfect solution to every problem, and if it is not found, the result will be terrible.* This idea is irrational because there are many possible solutions to most problems, but seldom is there any perfect solution. Each alternative solution has some good and some bad features. All we can really do is select one of the better alternatives and give it a try. If it doesn't work, we must try another. We live by doing the best we can in any set of circumstances. When we do this consistently, things seem to go well and catastrophes do not really beset us on every side. To hold out for perfection only causes needless anguish and often leads to worse solutions in the long run. If we hold out for perfection, decisions are often made by default. Seldom are these the best ones.

If we hold out for perfection, decisions are often made by default. Seldom are these the best ones.

12. *We have no control over our emotions; we are their victims, and cannot help how we feel.* In reality, we can exert a great amount of control over our feelings in many ways. If we work at it, especially through rational thinking, we can learn to control our emotions rather than being controlled by them.

13. *We have a right to expect a pain-free and trouble-free life; when we are not experiencing that, something is wrong.* Struggle, adversity, and suffering are part of nature. There is absolutely no reason to expect that we will be exempt. In reality, most people have more happy times than tribulations, but that is not a

The three major
categories of irrational
thinking:

1. I must perform well
and/or receive the
approval of significant
others, or else I am an
incompetent, unlovable
person.

2. You must treat me
kindly and fairly, or else
you are a rotten,
damnable individual.

3. Conditions must be
favorable and fortunate
(bringing me much gain
and little pain), or else
life is terrible, I can't
stand it, and it is hardly
worth living.

right. Furthermore, it does no good to fight against the nature of the universe when it causes us discomfort. Better to improve things as much as possible and accept philosophically what cannot be changed. For example, the death of a loved one is sad and unfortunate; but death is a part of life and we will all die. Each death must be accepted as a part of existence and the living must go on. Life is for the living.

14. *I know what is best for most people and if they would listen to me, things would be better.* The fact is that individuality is the most pleasant part of existence. No person is a carbon copy of another. If they were, that would be the real abnormality! Children must have limits to insure their safety, but the limits should be broad and they should have maximal freedom within the limits in order to grow and develop. By the time we become adults, we should make our own decisions and choices. We should tend to our business and allow others to do the same. This, of course, does not preclude joint decisions in areas where two or more people agree; but it is not good for one adult to force his or her will onto another. It seldom works and when it does, it is very destructive.

Ellis eventually concluded that there are three major categories of irrational thinking under which these specific ideas can be classified:

1. I must perform well and/or receive the approval of significant others, or else I am an incompetent, unlovable person.

2. You must treat me kindly and fairly, or else you are a rotten, damnable individual.

3. Conditions must be favorable and fortunate (bringing me much gain and little pain), or else life is terrible, I can't stand it, and it is hardly worth living.

Thinking about these categories of irrational thinking and employing the alternative principles of rational thinking protects us from much needless anxiety. Some people have found it helpful to get together with a friend or a group of friends and go over the principles of rational and irrational thinking together. Each can share experiences and examples of the principles and encourage the others to think and live rationally.

As the reader may have noticed, many of the rational principles are drawn from Stoic philosophy; those interested may want to read more of the Stoic philosophers. Some of Ellis's books, such as *A New Guide to Rational Living* (with Robert A. Harper) and *Growth through Reason,* are also helpful. Another book that is useful, though written mainly for depressed people, is *Feeling Good* by David D. Burns. Approaches similar to those just mentioned are currently referred to as *cognitive psychotherapy.* Aaron Beck and his colleagues have made major contributions to this area. One of Beck's books (with Gary Emery and Ruth Greenberg) is *Anxiety Disorders and Phobias: A Cognitive Perspective.*

STRESS MANAGEMENT EXERCISES

1. Pick from the list of 14 in this chapter the 3 irrational beliefs to which you are most prone, and dispute each of them by writing a paragraph of your own reasons that you know these beliefs to be false. Write the belief first; then write your reasons disputing it.

_____

_____

_____

_____

_____

_____

_____

_____

_____

_____

_____

_____

_____

_____

_____

_____

_____

_____

_____

_____

2. Write 2 or 3 irrational beliefs that cause you anxiety sometimes that are not in the list of 14. Then write your reasons why they are false. If you have trouble doing this because the beliefs seem so real to you, try writing what you would say to a friend if he or she, rather than you, had the beliefs.

_____

_____

_____

_____

_____

_____

_____

_____

_____

_____

_____

_____

_____

_____

_____

_____

_____

_____

3. Write down an irrational belief that you used to have, but no longer have. Write a paragraph about how and when you discarded that belief. What insights can you glean from this belief and the way you got over it?

_____

_____

_____

_____

_____

_____

_____

_____

_____

_____

_____

_____

_____

_____

_____

_____

_____

_____

_____

_____

4. Everyone has a catalog of cognitions, truisms, or sayings that help give direction to their behavior and that support them through stressful times. These are the opposite of irrational beliefs—they are truths that help in difficult times. For example, "This too will pass"; "You are never as good as your greatest success or as bad as your worst failure"; "Feeling inferior is the disease of the successful"; "You have to play the cards you are dealt"; and "Sometimes you have to do what you know is right, even if it doesn't make you popular." Assume that you are preparing young people to go out on their own in life. List five such truisms that you would tell these young people always to remember.

_____

_____

_____

_____

_____

_____

_____

_____

_____

_____

_____

_____

_____

5. Ask a couple of friends to make a list of their favorite truisms. Share your lists with each other.

_____

_____

_____

_____

3

Existential Anxiety
and Creative Living

*"Ultimately, man should
not ask what the meaning
of life is, but rather
recognize that it is he who
is asked."*
—VIKTOR FRANKL

IT IS ALMOST TRITE to comment on the rapid tempo of change in society today and on the growth of knowledge, technology, and affluence, but the fact is that the pace has quickened in the last generation or two. As someone has quipped, "If it works, it's obsolete." The world is changing so rapidly that children today are born into a world that literally will no longer exist when they are adults. They will be educated in school for tasks that shortly after they graduate will no longer need to be done. In years gone by things were more stable and predictable. The struggle for survival seemed to give intrinsic meaning to life, and goals seemed obvious. With the technology and affluence of today, however, mere survival is no longer such a struggle for most people in industrialized societies. In such circumstances, people begin to take stock of the meaning and quality of their existence. When they do, they often find themselves perplexed by questions such as, "Who am I? Where am I going? Why? What does it all mean? Does it really matter?" Intense anxiety and much anguish often accompany these questions.

Some psychotherapists have developed existential psychotherapy to help people deal with these questions and problems. One

33

of the more interesting pioneers in this field was the Viennese psychiatrist Viktor Frankl. Dr. Frankl would sometimes ask a despairing patient, "Why is it that you do not commit suicide?" With that jolting question, he was able to find a small corner from which to begin helping the patient find meaning in life. Frankl was well qualified to comment on the meaning of life. His ideas were tested when he was a prisoner in a German concentration camp during World War II. One of his early books was entitled *From Death Camp to Existentialism* (later revised and published as *Man's Search for Meaning*), and it led some people to think his ideas had originated in the camp. He once told me, however, that he had developed his ideas and had a manuscript for a book describing them before he was taken to the prison camp. His ideas were tested there, and he emerged more convinced of their truth than ever.

Frankl believed that the main motivation of human beings is to discover the meaning of existence. He referred to this as the *will-to-meaning* and contrasted it with the two other prevalent notions about the nature and motivation of humans. One notion is that we are motivated by seeking pleasure and avoiding pain; this hedonistic view he termed the *will-to-pleasure*. It is endorsed by many in different fields. In psychiatry, Sigmund Freud was one of the main exponents. The second theory of motivation is that humans are driven by a desire to master and conquer. This view was proposed by Alfred Adler, among others, and was characterized by Frankl as the *will-to-power*. Frankl thought that the latter views, each containing a grain of truth, were inadequate to describe the main motivating force in humans. The main force, he said, is the drive to understand the meaning of existence. This is what separates homo sapiens from other animals. Animals seek pleasure and conquest, but meaning is unknown to them. The essence of humans is meaning.

Frankl referred to the thwarting of one's will-to-meaning as *existential frustration*—frustration that grows out of an existential vacuum in one's life and manifests itself mainly in a state of boredom. There is a feeling of emptiness, a void within oneself, and the feeling that nothing is worthwhile. This state of boredom and void is not mental illness in and of itself. It is a disease of the spirit and is common to all people until they resolve it by discovering meaning in existence. If it persists, however, it is a fertile breeding ground for anxiety, neuroses, and other emotional problems.

Neuroses and emotional disturbances can, of course, arise from other causes, but today a large number of them develop out of existential vacuum and frustration. These are referred to by Frankl as *noogenic neuroses.* The word *noogenic* is made up of the word *noos,* which means "spirit," "soul," or "mind," and *genic,* which refers to "origin" or "beginning." These are neuroses that develop out of the problems of the spirit. Of course, many other emotional disturbances have an existential dimension in that they involve the spiritual dimension in one way or another. According to Frankl, a person cannot make life meaningful, nor can anyone else give one meaning for life; one must discover it. Others can help with this discovery.

Frankl called the system of psychotherapy that he developed to do this *logotherapy.* In this context, *logo* or *logos* refers to "meaning." The treatment helps a person discover meaning. Frankl was fond of quoting Nietzsche to the effect that one who has a *why* to live for can bear almost any *how.* Many of the ideas and techniques that Frankl developed can be used to help deal with the anxieties we often feel in life. Frankl pointed out that basic to being human is being conscious of and faithful to our responsibilities in life. Living our lives in such a way that we are responsible toward ourselves and toward others is the meaningful life. This is an ongoing process, not a status that we reach. Humans are not content when they reach homeostasis, or equilibrium, at which all pressures are absent. They are most content or happy, and life is most meaningful, when they are responsibly meeting and solving problems.

Life also has meaning when one is growing and progressing toward the achievement of values. There are three main areas of values: creative, experiential, and attitudinal. *Creative values* are realized when one works for the benefit of society. When we think

Living our lives in such a way that we are responsible toward ourselves and toward others is the meaningful life.

Life also has meaning when one is growing and progressing toward the achievement of values. There are three main areas of values: creative, experiential, and attitudinal.

of creative contributions, we generally think of such things as art, music, and literature. These are included in what Frankl means. A person seeking to realize such values might want to take up one of these endeavors as a pastime or as a profession. Most community colleges have courses that can get one started in them. The library, of course, has a wealth of information in such areas. There are also individuals and clubs in every community that can facilitate a person's becoming creative in everything from painting to wine-making or woodworking. Such achievement provides part of the meaning of life.

Creative values, however, are much broader than this. For example, doing a good job at work and being proud of the product, whatever it may be, are creative values. If we approach our daily jobs as a vehicle for expressing the creative values in life rather than putting in time to get a paycheck, we will discover a real and exciting dimension of existence that is all too often missed in the zombie-like work world. When we approach our work in such a manner, everyone profits. We have richer lives, and we enrich the existence of those around us. Creative values can be expanded even further. We can give of ourselves to others—friends, family, and neighbors. Putting a band-aid on a child's skinned knee and offering comfort is a very creative act. Working on community projects also can be. In creative achievement we find many of life's real meanings.

The second area is that of *experiential values*. This has to do with experiencing and appreciating such things as love, joy, curiosity, knowledge, nature, music, art, and history and so forth. Seeing the good, true, beautiful, interesting, and exciting in life leads to the discovery of depth and meaning. We do this by going to places where things are happening and becoming a part of them. We can attend concerts, visit art galleries, go to plays. Athletic events, if properly viewed, are a thrilling art form. Travel, reading, and a host of other activities could be included. There is an old joke about the man who spent a month one weekend in Waco, Texas (where the author lived, incidentally, when these lines were originally written). For a person who experiences and appreciates life, however, such a weekend could be an exciting adventure. Experiential values can also be realized by knowing a person in all of his or her uniqueness. Talking with and getting to know other human beings can be a remarkable experience if real communication occurs.

The third area, *attitudinal values,* has to do with facing life with the right attitudes. For example, if we can avoid suffering, we should; but if we are faced with unavoidable suffering, it can be a positive force in our lives. Suffering is ennobling if it is for a purpose and we bear up under it with strength. If our suffering contributes to another person or to an important cause, we are privileged to bear it. In one of his writings, Frankl tells of an old man who was despondent because his wife, whom he loved very much, had died. Frankl told the man that he was happy for him. The man replied, "How can you say that?" Frankl went on to point out to him that if he had died first, his wife would have known the grief. But because she had died first, he was privileged to bear the grief for her. We learn from suffering; tribulation is a fine instructor. The carefree life may be good, but the lessons of suffering lead to a personality of much greater depth and quality. Suffering can be a strong stimulus to growth and development. Thus, real meaning in life can often be found in suffering.

Another attitudinal value has to do with one's view of happiness. Frankl characterized the United States as being afflicted by "fun morality." We feel that the basic value and goal in life is to be happy and to have fun. This robs us of the significance of suffering in life because when we suffer we feel doubly bad. We feel bad because of the suffering, and we feel ashamed and bad because of our unhappiness. The right attitude toward happiness, however, is that it is not to be sought after, or even expected, all of the time. It is a by-product of living our lives in such a way that we fulfill their meaning and attain positive values. This is true happiness as opposed to mere fun.

Another attitudinal value concerns time. In his book *The Doctor*

Seeing the good, true, beautiful, interesting, and exciting in life leads to the discovery of depth and meaning.

Happiness is a by-product of living our lives in such a way that we fulfill their meaning and attain positive values.

and the Soul (2nd. ed. New York: Alfred A Knopf, 1972, pp. 33–34) Frankl includes the following comments on time:

> Time that has passed is certainly irrecoverable; but, what has happened within that time is unassailable and inviolable. Passing time is therefore not only a thief, but a trustee. Any philosophy which keeps in mind the transitoriness of existence need not be at all pessimistic. To express this point figuratively we might say the pessimist resembles a man who observes with fear and sadness that his wall calendar, from which he daily tears a sheet, grows thinner with each passing day. On the other hand, the person who takes life in the sense suggested above is like a man who removes each successive leaf from his calendar and files it neatly and carefully away with its predecessors—after first having jotted a few diary notes on the back. He can reflect with pride and joy on all the richness set down in these notes, on all the life he has already lived to the full. What will it matter to him if he notices that he is growing old? Has he any reason to envy the young people whom he sees, or wax nostalgic for his own youth? What reasons has he to envy a young person? For the possibilities that a young person has, the future that is in store for him? "No, thank you," he will think, "instead of possibilities, I have realities in my past—not only the reality of work done, but of love loved and of suffering suffered. These are the things of which I am most proud—though these are things which cannot inspire envy."

Your attitude toward your role in life is similarly important. Everyone has a unique destiny and contribution to make in life that nobody else can make. It is your responsibility to find that role and your duty to carry it out. Doing so gives meaning to life.

Death also gives meaning rather than destroying it. If life were not finite, everything could be put off until later. There would be no need for us to be active, to do, to accomplish. The fact that life

The fact that life must end makes the present significant.

must end makes the present significant. Thus, death is a part of life. It is sometimes interesting to approach a new day as though you were living it for the second time and had done it wrong the first time. This technique helps us see life in a new way. Living a life that expresses itself in the ways just outlined results in a life that has meaning. The person does not experience needless anxiety because of existential frustration.

There are also some specific techniques that Frankl developed and used with his patients. These techniques enable people to put things in perspective and enhances meaning in their lives. One is called *paradoxical intention*. Paradoxical intention is based on the theory that, in many cases, maladaptive behavior develops because a person is literally afraid of fear. That is, you think a certain situation will make you anxious, and then you become extremely frightened even of getting into that situation. This is called anticipatory anxiety, and it can escalate to disabling proportions. The fear of being frightened by a situation and the fear of the situation itself develop into a vicious circle that makes one avoid that situation as vigorously as possible. Such a person becomes overwhelmed with anxiety and is almost unable to function if actually forced into the situation. In using paradoxical intention in such a situation, you try to make the thing happen that you fear most in the situation. This is, of course, paradoxical. The pathogenic fear is replaced by a paradoxical wish. This technique takes the wind out of the sails of anticipatory anxiety, enabling the person to relax and handle the situation much more calmly.

A humorous example of this is offered by Frankl. He tells the story of a severe stutterer he treated as an adult. The man told him he had stuttered ever since he could remember. There was only one occasion when he didn't; it was when he was 12 years old. He hooked a ride on a streetcar and was caught by the conductor. He thought to himself that he would stutter and show the conductor that he was just a poor stuttering child. But when he tried to stutter, he was unable to do so. Another example from one of Frankl's colleagues concerned a man who had had a heart attack. He began to fear any sign of change in the rate of his heartbeat and was afraid to leave the hospital for fear that he might need medical attention at any moment of the day. When one of his anxiety attacks started, he was told to make his heart beat faster, increase the pain, and get as anxious as possible. The nurse then left him alone for a while. When she returned, he said he couldn't do it. In fact, the opposite happened: He now felt calm. This encouraged him enough to get up and take a walk outside the hospital, something he had not done for 6 months. In one of the shops he felt his heart begin to beat faster. He started saying to himself, "Try to feel even more anxiety." Again, he couldn't do it and actually became calmer. Soon after, he went home and returned to his job.

If one wanted to use this technique for the fear of public speaking, one might think just before getting up to speak, "I'm going to get as anxious as possible. I want anxiety and stage fright to flow through and envelop my whole body. I want to tremble and quake; to perspire and turn red; to stammer and stutter. I will be so anxious the whole building will tremble with me, and I'll probably drown the audience in perspiration. One thing is for sure, if the water doesn't get them, the odor will. I'll be the world's champion. Number one in stage fright. Do they have an Olympic category for that? If so, I will win the gold medal." Doing this will, paradoxically, make you calmer. It is important to ridicule the fear and use a sense of humor in deciding what you will say to yourself about the fear. This defuses the situation, making it possible for you to function more effectively.

According to Frankl, paradoxical intention relieves existential anxiety because it calls attention to the way we often focus on the trivial things in life and exaggerate them. This leads to irrational, unnecessary anxiety. If we call a halt to such nonsense and begin to concentrate on more meaningful things, we get rid of anxieties and live a more fulfilling, purposeful, and happier life. Paradoxical intention is a way of calling the bluff on these trivial fears. Of course, such fears thrive in an existential vacuum—so living a meaningful life is good protection from them.

It helps if we redirect our attention from the thing that is troubling us to some more meaningful value or to something of importance.

Another technique developed by Frankl is called *de-reflection*. De-reflection is somewhat similar to paradoxical intention. It is intended to counteract the obsessive-compulsive tendency we often develop toward self-observation. We begin by paying too much attention to something. The more we think about it, the worse the situation becomes. A good example is breathing. Try to watch your breathing and breathe normally. The more you try, the more your breathing becomes arrhythmic; the harder you try, the worse it gets. The same is true for insomnia. If you try to force yourself to go to sleep, you only ensure that you will stay awake. In the morning, when you give up because you have to get up, you fall asleep. It is possible to try too hard at some things, making success less likely than if you took it easier. In de-reflection the person is told simply to ignore the problem. Of course, many times this is easier said than done. It helps if we redirect our attention from the thing that is troubling us to some more meaningful value or to something of importance. Once we do this, we often find that this resolves the problem. It no longer causes us undue anxiety.

Frankl contrasts the right and wrong approaches to these techniques by talking about right and wrong passivity as well as right and wrong activity. *Wrong passivity* refers to withdrawal from situations as a result of anticipatory anxiety. It is a flight from fear. *Right passivity* is the use of paradoxical intention. Through this technique, the person stops fighting the situation but is able to become involved in it without fear or anxiety. *Wrong activity* is obsessively and compulsively dwelling on a problem or a concern until we are trying too hard and the goal becomes unattainable because of our overeffort. *De-reflection* is the right kind of activity in this situation. The person ignores the problem and redirects attention to more important things.

Some years ago Salvatore Maddi and Suzanne Kobasa became intrigued by the fact that some people break down under stress while others seem to thrive on it. They then had the opportunity to study a number of executives of the Bell Telephone Company.

Through their research, which they reported in a book called *The Hardy Executive: Health Under Stress,* they learned a great deal about people who handle stress well. Many of these people have inherited a favorable physiological constitution to withstand stress. They also have good health practices and a strong social network of friends and relatives that provide support. Of the greatest interest for our discussion here is the fact that these people also had personalities that transformed stress into the motivation to cope effectively with situations rather than letting stress defeat and debilitate them. The personality factors that were associated with this hardiness in the face of stress were tendencies toward (a) commitment and involvement, rather than withdrawal and alienation; (b) control, rather than powerlessness; and (c) seeing things as a challenge, rather than as a threat. Frankl would, no doubt, agree.

STRESS MANAGEMENT EXERCISES

1. If you asked yourself the question that Frankl used to ask his patients ("Why is it that you do not commit suicide?"), what would your answer be?

_____

_____

_____

_____

_____

_____

_____

_____

_____

2. What would give your life more meaning, and what can you do to make that a reality?

_____

_____

_____

_____

_____

_____

_____

_____

_____

_____

_____

_____

_____

_____

_____

_____

_____

_____

_____

_____

_____

_____

_____

3. Plan to read a book that will help you explore the meaning of life. Go to the library and browse around (the librarian will help if you tell him or her the nature of your assignment). You might choose a biography of a person who discusses his or her philosophy of life, or a philosophy book on the topic, or a collection of readings. List the title you choose and then summarize what you learned and your thoughts after reading the book.

_____

_____

_____

_____

_____

_____

_____

_____

_____

_____

_____

_____

_____

_____

_____

_____

_____

_____

_____

_____

_____

_____

_____

4. List three areas of your life in which you feel that you are very successful and three where you feel that you have been less successful than you wish. Develop a plan to increase your success in the three unsuccessful areas.

_____

_____

_____

_____

_____

_____

_____

_____

_____

_____

_____

_____

_____

_____

_____

_____

_____

_____

_____

_____

_____

_____

_____

_____

_____

_____

_____

5. To explore Frankl's concept of creative values, list the areas of your life in which you feel you are most creative. Then choose an area in which you would like to be more creative and develop a plan to accomplish this. For example, you might want to try your hand at painting, playing a musical instrument, or writing poetry or a novel. Write about your plan here.

_____

_____

_____

_____

_____

_____

_____

_____

_____

_____

_____

_____

_____

_____

_____

_____

_____

_____

_____

_____

_____

_____

6. To explore Frankl's experiential values, make a list of things you have always wanted to try, but never have gotten around to. Pick one from your list each month, and do it. Ask a friend to help you if one of your friends has experience in the area. Write out your list and check off the items as you do them.

_____

_____

_____

_____

_____

_____

_____

_____

_____

_____

_____

_____

_____

_____

_____

_____

_____

_____

_____

_____

_____

_____

_____

7. Regarding Frankl's concept of attitudinal values, pick an area in which you need to change your attitude in order to be able to achieve more meaning in life. Discuss it with a friend and write an essay about the way your attitude has changed as a result.

_____
_____
_____
_____
_____
_____
_____
_____
_____
_____
_____
_____
_____
_____
_____
_____
_____
_____
_____
_____
_____
_____
_____
_____
_____

8. Considering Frankl's concept of responsibility, list three areas in which you need to become more responsible and write a plan to accomplish this.

_____

_____

_____

_____

_____

_____

_____

_____

_____

_____

_____

_____

_____

_____

_____

_____

_____

_____

_____

_____

_____

_____

_____

_____

_____

_____

_____

9. What would you like people to say about you if you were suddenly to lose your life? Do you think they would say this? If not, what do you have to change in your life to make your wish a reality in the future? Write a plan to do this in the space following.

_____

_____

_____

_____

_____

_____

_____

_____

_____

_____

_____

_____

_____

_____

_____

_____

_____

_____

_____

_____

_____

_____

10. Compose an epitaph that you would like to be on your tombstone some day. What would you want to say there? Epitaphs range from admonitions to others ("Remember friend as you pass by, as you are now, so once was I; as I am now, so you must be; prepare for eternity and follow me") to humor ("Here lies Owen Moore—went away, owing more than he could pay"); from whimsical comments such as the one W. C. Fields supposedly suggested for his ("On the whole, I'd rather be in Philadelphia") to comments on a person's life, such as the inscription on the grave marker for Thomas Paine ("He lived long, done some good and much harm"). An interesting collection of epitaphs may be found in *Grave Matters* by E. R. Shushan, New York: Ballantine Books, 1990.

_____

_____

_____

_____

_____

_____

_____

_____

_____

_____

4

Life Structuring and Engineering

Often a lack of planning of our lives for the tasks we must accomplish subjects us to tensions, anxieties, and hassles.

OFTEN A LACK of planning of our lives for the tasks we must accomplish subjects us to tensions, anxieties, and hassles. Fortunately, many hassles are unnecessary and can be avoided easily through planning. Planning may be thought of as *structuring* or *engineering*. In structuring, we give organization to situations and set things up so that they will go smoothly. In engineering a situation, we develop a strategy of activity that will lead to a desired result.

Let's consider structuring first. Many times we are confronted with tasks that puzzle us in the sense that we cannot figure out exactly how we should proceed. We don't know where or how to start, which leads to anxiety and frustration. Often it results in our putting off doing anything about the task, which eventually leads to failure. If we can structure the situation clearly, we will get over the hump of inactivity. Then we have a good chance of successfully completing the task. For example, suppose our boss wants us to give a talk to a group of new employees at a professional dinner. This is a rather vague request, and in many companies it might be made over the phone or in a memo from the committee planning the program. Such a vague request may lead to considerable anxiety about what is expected and what to say.

We want to do a good job, especially in front of so many people, but we don't know really where to start.

If we structure the situation carefully, however, the task becomes much easier. To accomplish this, we might tell the person making the request that we need a little more information to make plans. We would then ask a number of questions such as, "What will have been covered in earlier meetings with the employees? What function is the talk to fulfill? How long should it be? Should it be light and entertaining or a more hard-hitting pep talk? Are there any points that should definitely be covered, or is the content entirely open? Do we have copies of talks given in previous meetings?" Once answers to questions of this type are obtained, the task becomes more manageable. The simple technique of structuring the situation keeps us from foundering and gets us started in the right direction.

It is also important to consider similar structuring questions about tasks we assign ourselves. If we think about what it is we are trying to accomplish, it will often help us to carry out the task efficiently, without undue anxiety and frustration. The basic principle of structuring applies to all sorts of tasks. Take, for example, a minor repair job around the house. If we think about what has to be done, plan a little, and see that we have the correct tools and materials at hand, the job can be fun. It is often enjoyable to putter around at small tasks. Poor structuring, however, results in frustration, anger, and failure because we discover in the middle that we don't have the correct tools or necessary materials.

Additional examples can be found in routine tasks that we must do every day. Many people lay out their clothes for the next day before they go to bed. They can sleep peacefully, and when they wake up in the morning they can get dressed and ready without having to make a lot of decisions or having to look for articles of clothing. I find it helpful to put things under my car keys if I don't want to forget them in the morning; that way I can't leave without seeing them. These are very simple techniques, but they can greatly reduce the number of daily hassles we need to manage.

Another common structuring technique that some people use is to keep track of appointments and duties by writing them on a calendar marked with the hours of the day for every day of the year. Calendars of this type are made small enough to carry in a pocket or keep on a desk—nowadays many people even keep a calendar of this type on a desktop computer or in a miniature pocket computer. Keeping such a calendar helps people structure their days and enables them to keep track of things; other people find such a system constraining. Using this method early in my career, I often failed to write everything down and kept forgetting to look at the calendar until it was too late. As a result I would miss appointments. At that time I found that it worked better for me to jot things down on small pieces of paper. I constantly made lists of things to do and wrote notes to myself about things I wanted to remember. I kept small pieces of blank paper handy at all times. They were on my desk, by my chair at home, in my wallet, by the bed, in my briefcase, and so on. When I needed to make a note or a list, I grabbed one of these and wrote on it. I then clipped them together and left them where I would see them. I put them in my pockets, in my shoes (so I'd see them in the morning), in my wallet (so I'd be reminded when I bought something), on my desk, and in similar places. Periodically, I sorted through my papers, threw the old ones away, put the important ones on top, and revised some. People were often amused by my system. It was messy, but it worked for me, and that is what counted. I virtually never missed another meeting or an appointment.

I remember reading about another professor who also used this system. Eventually his students caught on, and as a joke they began to write nonsense notes, which they put in his pockets and on his desk when he wasn't looking. He spent considerable time puzzling over what he had meant when he wrote those notes. Later in my career, I became adept at using the traditional appointment book and am looking forward to a small pocket computer for that purpose in the near future. However, I still make lists of things to do and write notes to remind myself of things I must remember.

My point in mentioning this is that writing things down reduces anxiety about forgetting them. Sorting through the papers tends to reduce tension and throwing papers away once the task is completed is very rewarding—not a bad payoff for a few pieces of scrap paper.

You can try many other small structuring techniques to make life more comfortable. Scheduling your departure for appointments with enough time so that you don't have to rush is one example. Of course, it's possible to get overly anxious about being on time, which is a different mistake. It is best simply to start out early enough to make it on time and establish a reputation for being punctual. Then, if on occasion you are late, you can take your time and not worry about it. Since you are usually on time, being a little late may be easily forgiven.

Life structuring can prevent many needless anxieties from ever arising. Thinking and planning in advance are the keys.

While one can become overly compulsive about such techniques, life structuring can prevent many needless anxieties from ever arising. Thinking and planning in advance are the keys. If we do that well, the event will be no problem when it occurs. Often when I'm coaching a student about a public presentation he or she is going to make, I tell the student to be sure to have an opening and a closing sentence in mind for the talk. Otherwise, he or she may get up and not know how to start the presentation or get to the end and discover there is no way to stop. The feeling of panic and growing embarrassment that develops as a public speaker in this situation struggles to get the first words out or continues to ramble at the end without a point can easily be avoided by planning the opening and closing in advance.

The same principle applies to many other areas of life. Planning and structuring prevent anxiety. At the University of Oklahoma Medical School we train many students in the health professions every year. The demands on them are heavy as they fulfill all of the tasks assigned. Every year when the new students arrive, our faculty write on the blackboard this message: "Remember, structure is your friend."

As I indicated at the outset, the engineering of life situations is also very important in reducing anxiety. Engineering involves a more complicated and active process than simply structuring. There are many situations that are very frustrating and cause significant anxiety. With some forethought, however, it is often possible to engineer the problems out of the situation. A good example of this is how to solve the common problem of Sunday neurosis. Many people find the week very hectic and look forward to the relaxation of the weekend; and often the weekend starts out all right, and they do feel some relief. By Sunday afternoon, however, they begin to feel depressed, anxious, and at loose ends. They are miserable—they just don't know what to do with themselves. They find themselves desperately wishing it was Monday morning so they could go back to work and get over their distress. This is unfortunate, of course, because Sunday afternoon and evening can be a very enjoyable time. Most people do not relax nearly enough, and this opportunity should not be wasted.

An effective way to deal with Sunday neurosis is to engineer it out of existence. The way to do this is a relatively simple task. Plan some activity that you ordinarily enjoy but don't get around to doing very often, and do it during that time. Take the family for a ride. Go to the beach. Go on a picnic. Invite some friends over to watch a football game or for dinner. Work on a hobby. Go to a concert. See a movie (or two if you wish). Visit relatives. Browse around the library or used book store, or the Internet. There are a thousand things to indulge in; doing so will make the work week more enjoyable because you can look forward to the days off. It will make the weekend itself more enjoyable by helping you to relax and have some pleasant recreation. Make sure the activity selected is one that is relaxing, that you sincerely enjoy, and that adds a pleasant dimension to your life. Usually if you do this for a few weeks, the problem of Sunday neurosis disappears. At that point, it is not necessary to plan a major activity every Sunday, but occasional activities will continue to be very enjoyable.

If we frequently feel the effects of rather intense Sunday neurosis, and if our attempts at engineering do not prove very successful, it may be that our lives hold unresolved problems that we crowd out by keeping busy during the week. When we finally slow down, these problems surface and the feelings are depressing. If this is the case, it is wise to think about and work out solutions to these problems either on our own or with help from a friend or a professional counselor. Many times, however, Sunday neuroses are not that deep or complicated. They result from the contrast between the high-adrenalin week and the reduced pace of the weekend, which results in reduction of adrenalin and negative feelings.

Another example of engineering can be found in the area of entertaining house guests. Most people are fairly adept at this and do a good job at engineering this rather simple situation. Yet many others have problems with it and become very anxious when called on to entertain guests at home. Even those who do not have much trouble in this area may have trouble if the guests are unusually important or threatening in some way.

Proper engineering in this situation calls for deciding what type of entertaining you wish to do—Is it to be a large cocktail party or a small dinner party? Will it be for old friends or for people who have not previously met? A number of similar questions might be asked. Once some basic decisions are made, you can begin to engineer the situation so that anxiety will be unlikely to occur. You need to consider the evening from start to finish and arrange things so they will go smoothly. For example, if it is to be a small dinner party, you may already know whether any of the guests have specific dietary requirements due to health problems or strong personal likes or dislikes. If you do not know, it is a good idea to check this with each guest. With this information, it will be possible to plan a menu, which might involve food that is not highly risky in terms of the possibility of turning out badly and that can be prepared, to a considerable extent, ahead of time. The guests should be chosen so that they will enjoy one another's company and will be able to keep a lively conversation going. Structured activities such as listening to one of the guests sing or play a musical instrument can be planned to add to the evening. Although these are only a few examples, planning of this type will have the effect of engineering anxiety out of such situations. It is better to engineer situations in this manner and keep anxiety from growing out of proportion than to either avoid them or endure them with great pain.

After we have had some successful experiences, the planning and engineering will not need to be so elaborate. Much of it will become automatic, and we won't even have to think about it. The same general point can be made about all of the suggestions in this chapter. They may seem elaborate and overdrawn, but the point is that they should be used to reduce anxiety and hassles in situations that often upset us. If we don't need them in certain situations, then no purpose is served by using them. We all have situations that just seem to be hard for us to handle; structuring and engineering can often make them easier to manage. The exact situations that need this type of planning and the specific techniques used with it will vary from person to person, depending on lifestyle, what seems to work, and what you are comfortable with, but anxiety can be planned out of existence with proper structuring and engineering. A good idea is to talk with a friend whom you know to be good at handling the situation that troubles you. Get your friend's advice on planning and then review your plans with that person before the event. It is amazing how much can be learned this way.

One of the most important areas in which these methods may be necessary is that of time management. Most of us never seem to have enough time to do all the things we want. As a result, we go through life wishing we had more time for activities that we really enjoy, while spending a great deal of time on things that we don't enjoy. Recently there have been a number of articles and books written on the topic of how to manage time. When you think about it, time is certainly the most precious possession we have. Benjamin Franklin once said, "To love life is to love time, because time is the stuff of which life is made." If we learn some of the techniques of time management, we will find that it is possible to get all of the work done that must be done and still have

It is better to engineer situations in this manner and keep anxiety from growing out of proportion than to either avoid them or endure them with great pain. Anxiety can be planned out of existence with proper structuring and engineering.

considerable time left for other activities. One of C. N. Parkinson's basic laws is that work will expand or contract to fill the time that one has to perform it (*Parkinson's Law and Other Studies in Administration*).

Time management is half philosophy and half technique. With modern technology, we have an infinite number of possibilities on which to spend time. We can travel most anywhere in the world in a few hours, read millions of publications free from the library, watch thousands of TV programs or movies at will, contact anyone in the world by telephone in seconds (or at least talk to their machine), and spend hours on the Internet. Yet, philosophically, we must accept that we cannot do everything. Thus, we must use certain techniques to make choices and be comfortable with the idea that we are saying no to others. The techniques of time management have to do with ways to do things more efficiently, thus saving time to do other things that we want to do.

The first step in time management is to analyze everything that we do at work and at home each day of the week. We should consider each activity in light of whether or not we want to continue devoting time to it. A good question to ask about an activity is, "What will happen if I don't do this?" Most people find that many activities they perform don't really matter. If they don't really matter, don't do them. Do something that makes a difference. For the remaining activities, arrange them in a daily priority list. Each day, work through the list as far as possible. Most of us will never get through the whole list in a given day, but we will generally get through the top three or four items. Those left over can be considered with respect to their inclusion on the list for the next day and their ranking on that list. By using this system, we make certain that we do the important things and do not waste time on unimportant activities.

As we analyze our duties we may also discover that it is possible to delegate some of them. A good rule is to delegate any activity that you don't like to do and that is fair or reasonable to delegate. One of the most certain ways to waste time and be so exhausted that you cannot do the things you want to do is to try to do every-

The first step in time management is to analyze everything that we do at work and at home each day of the week.

A good rule is to delegate any activity that you don't like to do and that is fair or reasonable to delegate.

thing yourself. It is also a good idea to purchase services for things you don't want to do as long as they're affordable. I have a colleague who is a highly accomplished professional and who keeps a busy schedule in her work. She often invites people to dinner, but I have never known her to cook anything. She purchases delicious items from selected delicatessens and assembles a feast, but does not waste time or put herself under undue stress by trying to prepare a major meal for guests. Everyone, including the hostess, has an excellent and relaxing time. Similarly, you can treat guests to a meal in a favorite restaurant rather than cooking at home. A more common example of purchasing services, of course, is the use of a housekeeper when both partners work and have little time for housework. Many others could be mentioned. It goes without saying that all family members should take on a fair share of household chores; the remaining chores are purchased.

Time management also involves becoming more efficient at everything we do. To become more efficient, we should think about each task we do and consider whether there is a better way to do it than the way we have gone about it in the past. Often we will immediately spot a better way; other times we may need to ask those who seem to be more efficient than we are in that area. With a little thought, most of the things we do daily can be done more efficiently. For example, if we wish to shop for an item and compare prices, we can get in the car and go from store to store. Yet many items can be compared readily, at least initially, by calling each store on the phone to get a description of the product and the price. We may then only have to actually go and inspect two or three items before making our purchase, rather than visiting several stores that don't carry the product or have a product that is unsuitable. Price comparison and shopping also can be done very efficiently by computer.

It is also possible to use the telephone in place of personal meetings or appointments. It is amazing that business that can be transacted in 5 to 10 minutes over the phone would generally take 30 minutes to an hour in a face-to-face meeting. A phone call is often much quicker and more efficient than a letter or memo.

The FAT system:
File it.
Act on it.
Throw it away.

Another example of efficiency that many people learn is that if we get in the habit of cleaning up after ourselves each time we do something, it never takes several hours of cleaning to put the house or office in order. Likewise, it is possible to double recipes when cooking and freeze part for a later meal, cutting down on cooking time. Similar strategies work very well in the office. Some people use the *FAT system* of dealing with mail. If you need to keep something, *File it.* If you need to do something about it, *Act on it* (write a response or make a call) immediately. If you don't need to do either, *Throw it away.* A good general principle in office work is to finish each task as you work on it, if at all possible. Going back later doubles the amount of time the task takes. The chair of our department at the medical school used to write memos in the presence of the person requesting them; he would pick up his dictating unit and dictate the memo on the spot. This accomplished several things at once. First, at the end of a day of appointments, he was finished. He did not have several hours of dictation to do. Second, the person in question could correct him if he was misstating the point or could supply information needed to complete the case. Third, the person requesting the memo was certain it had been written and knew exactly what it said. Over the years, I have encouraged students to write their clinical notes during the session with the patient (or immediately after). That way, the task is complete. This helps them avoid hours of note writing at the end of the day when memory has already begun to dim.

Choosing the best way to handle tasks is important. Many people, in an attempt to be efficient, indulge in overkill and actually waste time. I have known people who, having spent hours looking for a receipt in order to return an item to the store, developed an elaborate system of classifying and filing all receipts. This is actually a waste of time because most of them will never be needed. The system I use is to throw receipts in a drawer if there is any chance I will be returning the item. If I need the receipt, I know where it is and I know approximately what depth it will be in the pile based on how long ago the purchase was made. It does not take long to find it. Periodically, I sift through the bottom layer and throw unneeded receipts away. This system takes virtually no time or effort and is very effective. A caution about computers is in order here. Computers are wonderful machines to store and manipulate data—however, sometimes they are more time consuming than simpler systems for handling the same information.

Another element of efficiency is choosing the time to do a task and making whatever arrangements are necessary to avoid interruption until it is done. I've heard one woman describe her job as a series of interruptions interrupted by other interruptions. Nobody can function efficiently under such circumstances. Schedule specific times for tasks, and resist unnecessary interruptions by whatever means possible.

One final time-management principle that has a great stress-reduction effect is, "If a crisis happens more than once, it should be planned out of existence." Much time is wasted dealing with crises, and crises obviously increase our stress. Yet most crisis situations can be anticipated and their effects greatly reduced by planning. Emergency rooms in hospitals have all of the supplies and instruments necessary for specific emergencies prepared and packaged in advance. When a person is brought to the emergency room, the staff simply retrieves the appropriate packet and attends to the patient. If they began their search for each individual necessary item when the patient arrived, the result could be disastrous.

Some useful books for those interested in more information on time management are *Hour Power,* by Lee Pierce with John W. Lee; *The Management of Time,* edited by A. Dale Timpe; *How to Get Control of Your Time and Your Life,* by Alan Lakein; *If You Haven't the Time to Do it Right, When Will You Find the Time to Do it Over?* by Jeffrey J. Mayer; *The Complete Idiot's Guide to Managing Your Time,* by Jeff Davidson; *The Ten Natural Laws of Successful Time and Life Management,* by Hyrum Smith; *Time Management for Dummies,* by Jeffrey Mayer; *Time Management for the Creative Person,* by Lee Silber; *How to be Organized in Spite of Yourself,* by Sunny Schlenger and Roberta Roesch; and, *Organizing from the Inside Out,* by Julie Morgenstern.

STRESS MANAGEMENT EXERCISES

1. On the left side of this page make a list of your top 10 priorities in life. On the right side list the things you spent the most time on in the last month. What differences do you see between the two lists? What can you do about it?

Priorities	Time Spent

2. List below some ways you structure things in your life to reduce stress. Ask a friend to do the same. Compare lists and see what you can learn from each other.

_____

_____

_____

_____

_____

_____

_____

_____

_____

_____

_____

_____

_____

_____

_____

_____

_____

_____

_____

_____

_____

_____

_____

_____

_____

3. Pick a couple of areas in your life that need to be better structured. Develop a plan to achieve this. Get ideas from friends if you have trouble coming up with creative ideas. Write your plan here.

_____

_____

_____

_____

_____

_____

_____

_____

_____

_____

_____

_____

_____

_____

_____

_____

_____

_____

_____

_____

_____

_____

_____

_____

_____

4. Review your system for tracking important events in your life (e.g., appointments, birthdays, anniversaries, etc.) and decide if it is working. If not, develop a better system and write an outline of the new system in this space.

_____

_____

_____

_____

_____

_____

_____

_____

_____

_____

_____

_____

_____

_____

_____

_____

_____

_____

_____

_____

_____

_____

_____

_____

_____

_____

5. Consider your filing system. Reorganize your system if it needs it. Purge old obsolete material from your files. Some people put all purged material in a box which they keep in the attic or garage for one to two years before finally throwing it away. That way they don't accidentally throw things away that they may need. Remember that the IRS expects you to keep records for at least three years. Make some notes about how to reorganize your files in the following space.

_____

_____

_____

_____

_____

_____

_____

_____

_____

_____

_____

_____

_____

_____

_____

_____

_____

_____

_____

_____

_____

_____

_____

6. Pick one area in your life that needs to be better engineered to reduce stress. Write down a plan to do that. Often, the type of situations in need of engineering are ones for which others share responsibility. If this is the case, call a meeting of all persons involved and have a brain storming meeting about how to improve the situation.

_____

_____

_____

_____

_____

_____

_____

_____

_____

_____

_____

_____

_____

_____

_____

_____

_____

_____

_____

_____

_____

_____

_____

_____

7. Pick three areas in which better time management is needed in your life. Write your plan for better management in each of these areas.

_____

_____

_____

_____

_____

_____

_____

_____

_____

_____

_____

_____

_____

_____

_____

_____

_____

_____

_____

_____

_____

_____

_____

_____

_____

_____

8. Pick an area of your life in which you have a recurring crisis (tax time, getting to work on time, etc.) and prepare a "crisis plan" or "crisis packet" that will prevent the crisis from occurring again. For example, the tax-time crisis may involve developing a better record keeping and storage system, as well as planning time to prepare the tax form before the due date, or it might require the purchase of services such as having a professional tax person prepare your form. The getting-to-work-on-time crisis can be solved by setting a goal to be at work a few minutes before starting time. Then, if an unexpected delay occurs, there is a buffer to prevent being late—and if one is occasionally late but is usually there a couple of minutes early, the lateness is generally overlooked. Write down your crisis and the plan to prevent it.

_____

_____

_____

_____

_____

_____

_____

_____

_____

_____

_____

_____

_____

_____

_____

_____

_____

_____

_____

_____

9. Review all of the tasks you perform regularly and make a list of those that can be delegated. List the task and to whom you will delegate it.

_____

_____

_____

_____

_____

_____

_____

_____

_____

_____

10. Read one or two of the books mentioned at the end of this chapter and make some notes of things you learned from the books.

_____

_____

_____

_____

_____

_____

_____

_____

_____

_____

_____

_____

_____

_____

5

Realistic Goal Setting

SOME PEOPLE JUST drift along with the tide. They don't seem to have any goals and their lives appear to lack direction. As a result, they don't achieve much. Often they are very capable and talented individuals. People who know them frequently lament the tragedy that they are not more goal-directed and more productive.

At the other extreme are people who constantly set *very* high goals for themselves. In fact, they set such high goals that it is impossible to achieve them. These people are chronically tense and miserable because they are constantly failing. Every unachieved goal is a failure. Even goals that they achieve but that took longer than they had planned are regarded as failures. Such people drive themselves relentlessly. Often they accomplish a great deal, but they don't enjoy it. The fact that they didn't accomplish as much as they had wanted to as soon as they had hoped robs them of any pleasure in their achievements. After a time they find their energy sapped by this tension. They become disillusioned with their goals and frequently grow cynical and depressed.

Both of these types of individuals suffer from the same basic problem: They are unable to formulate realistic goals to guide their lives. The one who drifts with the tide commonly sets either very low goals or no goals at all because of fear and anxiety. He or she is afraid to fail and knows that failure will cause anxiety; therefore, he or she does not set goals. The second type of person sets goals that are too high; as we have seen, this also results in defeat because failure is built in from the start.

In addition to setting goals that are too high or too low, we can set goals for ourselves that are faulty. This, likewise, leads to disaster. When we do this, we find ourselves expending a great deal of energy and time to achieve something, only to discover that it was not what we wanted in the first place. Sometimes it is not possible to detect faulty goals in advance, but often, if we examine our values and think about the goal, we can determine whether we really want it.

When couples come to me for marriage counseling, the subject of divorce frequently arises. Many times the partners are sure that they want a divorce. They think they could be happy if only they could get rid of their lousy partners. I ask them to think about it a bit and tell me how many things actually would be different and in what ways they would be different if they were no longer married to their partners. Sometimes when they do this they realize that they have been blaming their partners for everything unpleasant in their lives, and if they are honest, they realize that the real causes lie elsewhere. Divorce in such cases is a faulty goal; in other cases, of course, it may be a very legitimate one.

The task is to set good, realistic goals for ourselves. Such goals can give direction to our lives and a feeling of accomplishment when we achieve them, and can help us be successful, productive people.

To better understand the process of setting goals we need to consider both long-range and short-range goals. *Long-range goals* are major things we want to accomplish eventually in our lives. *Short-range goals* are the things we have to do more or less immediately; they are the tasks that we set for ourselves to accomplish each day. Long-range goals are generally achieved by accomplish-

Sometimes it is not possible to detect a faulty goal in advance, but often, if we examine our values and think about the goal, we can determine whether we really want it.

ing many short-range goals. For example, a high school student's wanting to be a teacher is a long-range goal. Short-range goals toward that end would include passing tests and completing assignments in the necessary courses in college, accumulating a sufficient number of credit hours, obtaining a college degree, becoming certified as a teacher, and finding a teaching job.

There are rules that, when followed, enable one to set good long- and short-range goals. With regard to setting a long-range goal, you must first decide whether the goal is an appropriate one. Watch out for those that are too high, too low, or possibly faulty; careful consideration of all relevant information will serve as a guide. It also helps to talk to others and learn from their experiences. Get good advice from friends and/or professionals about whether the potential goal is a good, realistic one for a person such as yourself. In the end, however, only you can make the decision. This can be difficult because, while there are some things we just can't do (the person writing this paragraph stands 5 feet 6 inches tall and would not be well advised to seek a career as a center in the NBA), history is replete with people who overcame seemingly overwhelming odds to achieve their goals. The important thing is to be realistic but then go for it if you think you can do it.

Second, make long-range goals that are general rather than specific. If they are too specific, we almost always set ourselves up for failure. If they are more general, we'll find that they can be achieved in a number of ways, and we can be content with a number of accomplishments. It is better to set the goal of being an educated person and going as far as circumstances permit in college training than to make the goal of obtaining a PhD from Harvard with a straight-A average. It is better to set a goal of being a good contributor to community betterment than to decide that you must be voted the most outstanding citizen by some club and be elected the youngest mayor the city has ever had. Goals that are too specific almost always are frustrated and lead to a feeling of failure. Even when achieved, they are often found to be hollow and false.

There are rules that, when followed, enable one to set good long- and short-range goals.

Third, once a long-range goal is selected, carefully analyze it to determine the exact short-range goals that must be accomplished to get there. Plan the path of short-range sub-goals most likely to lead successfully to the long-range goal for you. There is always more than one way to achieve a given long-range goal; you don't have to do it the way somebody else did. You need to go about it in the way that is most likely to lead to success for you, with your strengths, weaknesses, and personality.

Things that are worthwhile take time.

Fourth, start working systematically on the short-range goals, and be patient. Things that are worthwhile take time. Set up a time schedule that is realistic, then allow yourself half again that amount of time before you begin to worry about not making progress. People with goals they are eager to achieve nearly always underestimate the length of time it will take to accomplish them. To the old saying, "Rome wasn't built in a day, you know," such people would retort, "Yes, but I wasn't foreman on that job." Things always seem to go slower than we'd hoped. I remember one of my research assistants telling me one day that he had discovered a basic principle of research. I asked him what it was. He replied, "Things take longer than they do." The point is, we must be patient with goals. Otherwise we set ourselves up for chronic frustration, tension, and anxiety.

The following rules are helpful in setting short-range goals. First, as with long-range goals, short-range goals should be realistic. They should be small, discrete steps toward the long-range goal. They should be things we can do more or less immediately and that will move us along toward the long-range goal.

Second, they should be more specific than the long-range goals. They should be sufficiently specific to enable us to know what we want to accomplish next and where we are going. Otherwise we will find ourselves standing around *thinking* that we want to get closer to the long-range goal but making no real progress because we don't know what to do next.

Third, our approach to accomplishing these short-range goals should be planned and organized in such a way that we have a high likelihood of getting them done (the ideas presented in Chapter 4 can be put to work here).

Fourth, if we fail at one short-range goal, we should not make more of that failure than it really is. We often catastrophize at such times and behave as though one false step meant we'd never make it to the ultimate goal—which is rarely, if ever, true. If we fail at a short-range goal, we should back up and try it again, or we should figure out an alternate route that will get us around the barrier. We should not let minor setbacks depress us; they are to be expected and overcome. They are all part of the process.

When you achieve a short-range goal, celebrate it. Celebrate liberally as you go along. Psychologists would refer to this as reinforcement or as rewarding yourself for desired behavior. Whatever you call it, it is very effective. The celebration can be a small thing or something bigger. For example, if you are studying for an exam, you can put some nuts or candy or a soft drink on the table. The material to be studied can then be divided into very small units—pages, sections of chapters, or basic concepts. As each unit is completed, you can reward yourself with a piece of candy or a sip of the soft drink. It is important to keep the study units small and reward yourself with small amounts of the candy or drink frequently; massive rewards after massive amounts of work are less successful. If you try this, you will find that studying goes a lot faster and is much more enjoyable. This basic idea can be applied to all sorts of tasks. It is a simple technique, but amazing in its effectiveness.

Of course, the celebration can also be more major for accomplishing a more important short-range goal or for the final accomplishment of a long-range goal. Thus, completion of a course or a semester might call for dinner at an expensive restaurant, a short vacation trip, or a gift for ourselves. Use of this approach makes getting there half the fun. People who arrange their lives this way enjoy themselves and what they are doing a little more.

Once the long-range and short-range goals have been considered and established, it is best to shift our attention and empha-

When you achieve a short-range goal, celebrate it.

sis to the *process*. The goals should be carried lightly. If we fix our attention on them too firmly, we will find ourselves so future-oriented that we never enjoy the present—always going somewhere but never arriving. Looking forward too much to future goals makes us unhappy with the present moment and tempts us to make excessive sacrifices to get to our goals. When we get to those goals, however, we always establish new ones and begin the process over. In that way we never enjoy living in the present, because we are preparing to enjoy the future, and that future never comes.

Looking forward too much to future goals makes us unhappy with the present moment and tempts us to make excessive sacrifices to get to our goals.

Goals are for direction and planning. After they have been established, we need to put them in the backs of our minds and begin to concentrate on the process, which means immersing ourselves in and thoroughly enjoying what we are doing now, not just as a means to an end but as an experience in and of itself. If we have our direction set by goals and throw ourselves wholeheartedly into the process of living and doing, we are most likely both to enjoy our lives and to achieve our goals. As in many areas of life, we can go too far in either extreme; it is the right balance that is most satisfying.

Of course, saying we are not going to think about our goals too much is easier than actually doing so. To keep the goals and process in perspective we need to be mentally vigilant and refuse to let ourselves become preoccupied with them. We can do this by working at being patient and by forcing ourselves not to think about them too much. A technique that often works in helping prevent obsessive preoccupation with goals is to write them down on a piece of paper or in a notebook. Just writing them down reassures us that we have them figured out and that they won't be forgotten, so that we need not be mentally vigilant about them anymore. Having them on paper relieves us of that.

Many people get their notebooks out from time to time, read over their lists of goals, and fantasize or project themselves into the future. They let their minds wander and think about what it will be like when they reach certain goals and the things they will do along the way to achieve them. Such fantasies are useful because they keep us motivated and often serve as a type of planning session. Using such fantasy sessions frees us to think about other things in between.

If you still have trouble with preoccupation with unachieved goals, a technique called thought stopping might help. *Thought stopping* is an anxiety-reducing technique that is used to get rid of obsessive ideas or thoughts that sometimes run through the mind incessantly. In using the thought-stopping technique you should get the thought that has been a problem firmly in mind. You then shout very loudly, "Stop! Stop! Stop!" You may pound your fist on the table for emphasis. This is repeated several times. Next, you practice saying "Stop" mentally while pounding with your fist for emphasis. Then you practice saying it mentally while thinking about pounding your fist. Later, when the thought occurs during the day, you say "Stop!" in your mind and imagine pounding your fist. After doing that, you should think of or do something else that is absorbing and interesting. This rather simple technique is often very effective in ridding a person of obsessive thoughts. If you have this problem in any area, you might want to give it a try.

Sometimes, if the thought is only mildly obsessive, you can skip the part about shouting "Stop!" and pounding your fist. You can just emphatically say to yourself, "I'm not going to think about that now." Following this, think about or do something else.

One final word about goal setting. In setting goals, *flexibility* is a very important point to keep in mind. Goals, once set, should not be looked on as musts. With time, circumstances change, and we change. What may have been a good goal when originally formulated may not be such a good idea at a later date. Therefore, it is necessary to be flexible and willing to change goals once in a while. This can be done as we go along, day by day. Some people use the leisure of vacation time to take a trip and reevaluate goals with more time to think them through. Sometimes we reach an important point along the way that can serve as an occasion to reassess the goal. We may choose to continue on, to change it

Thought stopping *is an anxiety-reducing technique that is used to get rid of obsessive ideas or thoughts.*

In setting goals, flexibility *is a very important point to keep in mind.*

slightly, or even to abandon it in favor of some other goal that now seems better. There is only so much time in life, and we can't do everything we might like. A friend of mine used to say, "We do what we do at the expense of something else we might have done." This fact makes goal setting and periodic goal revision crucial.

STRESS MANAGEMENT EXERCISES

1. The process of goal setting is facilitated by taking inventory. List three areas of your life in which you feel a significant sense of success or accomplishment.

_____

_____

_____

_____

_____

_____

_____

_____

_____

_____

_____

2. Now, write down one area of your life in which you feel less successful. Develop a plan to improve in this area. Repeat this process for other areas, if you wish.

_____

_____

_____

_____

_____

_____

_____

_____

_____

_____

_____

_____

_____

_____

_____

_____

_____

3. Write in the following space a dream that you would like to accomplish (e.g., I would like to take a trip around the world . . . to become a teacher . . . own my own home).

_____

_____

_____

_____

_____

_____

_____

_____

_____

_____

4. Convert the dream in item 3 into a long-range goal (e.g., for the trip around the world, get information on world tours, how much they cost, where they go, and so forth—then pick the type that interests you). Write your findings in the space provided.

_____

_____

_____

_____

_____

_____

_____

_____

_____

_____

_____

_____

5. Test the goal using the concepts discussed in this chapter. Is it possible for you? Is the concept too specific? How long would it take you to accomplish it? Are problems or risks involved?

_____

_____

_____

_____

_____

_____

_____

_____

_____

_____

_____

_____

_____

_____

_____

_____

_____

_____

_____

6. Develop a set of short-range sub-goals that will help you achieve your long-range goal. For example, do you need to develop a systematic savings program, get a part-time job, borrow money, sell assets? Are there ways to get discount tours, or to travel at no cost by working your way? Explore all the possibilities. Talk to people who have done it or know how to do it in the best way. Visit the library or the Internet for information. Make a list of sub-goals (be very specific) and set dates by which you can realistically accomplish them—then give yourself half again as much time.

_____

_____

_____

_____

_____

_____

_____

_____

_____

_____

_____

_____

_____

_____

_____

_____

_____

_____

_____

_____

7. Begin to work the plan you have developed. Consider working with one or more partners; involving another person increases motivation and spreads the work load around. Celebrate each sub-goal achieved and mark it off of the list above. List possible partners in the space following.

_____

_____

_____

_____

_____

_____

_____

_____

_____

8. Daydream about what it will be like when you achieve your goal. Project yourself mentally into the future and fantasize the experience. Write your thoughts down, then get back to work on the sub-goals.

_____

_____

_____

_____

_____

_____

_____

_____

_____

_____

9. What was a past dream or goal of yours that you no longer hold? Why is it no longer a goal? Are you happy with that or do you need to rediscover old goals and make them realities? Write down your thoughts.

_____

_____

_____

_____

_____

_____

_____

_____

_____

_____

_____

_____

6

Relaxation Exercises

EVERYONE WHO HAS gazed at the product of a bodybuilding program or who has watched a skilled athlete perform has been impressed with what can be done to develop and train the muscles of the body through regular, diligent practice. Recent developments in the field of psychology indicate that considerable conscious control can also be exerted over basic physiological processes that were previously thought to be more or less automatic and not subject to such intentional control. Patients have been taught to control heart rate, blood pressure, body temperature, brain waves, and other functions through training. The technique is generally referred to as *biofeedback;* its basic strategy is to arrange for the individual to receive some type of recognizable feedback when the body process is changing in the desired direction and a different type of feedback when it isn't. For example, if you were trying to relax, you might have an apparatus attached that would monitor muscle tension and indicate by a sound what the muscle was doing. Typically the muscle on the forehead is used because it is easy to connect to the electrodes and provides a fairly good index of overall muscle tension. If tension in the muscle begins to increase, the sound becomes louder and faster. As the muscle relaxes, the sound becomes softer and slower. By giving the person this kind of feedback it is rather easy to train a person to relax, which of course, is very worthwhile.

Use of biofeedback techniques does require expensive equipment and highly trained personnel to operate it. Fortunately, it is possible to train yourself to relax your muscles without either; you can learn to do it easily on your own. If relaxation procedures are practiced with regularity, your levels of tension and anxiety can be reduced significantly. These procedures may be thought of as relaxation exercises. Just as physical exercise trains and strengthens the muscles, making it possible for us to accomplish physical activities that we could not do otherwise, relaxation exercises increase our ability to tolerate stress and to remain calm in the face of life's pressures and problems.

Relaxation exercises increase our ability to tolerate stress and to remain calm in the face of life's pressures and problems.

The nervous system does not increase in size or change in the same way muscles do with exercise; but with a program of relaxation exercises, the nervous system's functional capacity does change in a similar way. Many anxious people feel fairly well in the morning but find themselves becoming more and more tense as the day wears on. By the end of the day they are so tied in knots that they can't enjoy an evening meal. They later find themselves sitting in agony in front of the TV with heartburn, muscular tightness, nausea, a splitting headache, and a general feeling of pain and discomfort. They are unable to relax.

What causes this is that during the day minor threats and problems generate tension and anxiety. This makes some people uncomfortable and makes them worry about the fact that they are not feeling well and whether there will be more threats and problems as the day wears on, and tomorrow, and next week. . . . They begin to wonder if they will be able to cope with them indefinitely. Thus, problems, tension, and worry develop into a closed-loop system that maintains itself rather than being dissipated. The net result is a spiral effect, with anxiety increasing at a steady pace, until it is almost unbearable by the end of the day.

To stop this process it is necessary to interrupt the feedback, thus breaking the spiral. One of the simplest ways to accomplish this is to use a basic relaxation procedure through which you learn to relax completely. Believe it or not, you can actually train yourself to do this rather easily. First, sit in a comfortable chair or lie on a couch or bed. Then say something like the following to yourself:

"I am going to relax completely. I will relax my forehead and scalp. I will let all the muscles of my forehead and scalp relax and become completely at rest. All of the wrinkles will smooth out of my forehead and that part of my body will relax completely. Now I will relax the muscles of my face. I will just let them relax and go limp. There will be no tension in my jaw. Next I will relax my neck muscles. Just let them become tranquil and allow all of the pressure to leave them. My neck muscles are relaxing completely. Now I will relax the muscles of my shoulders. That relaxation will spread down my arms to the elbows, down the forearms to my wrists, hands, and fingers. My arms will just dangle from the frame of my body. I will now relax the muscles of my chest. I will take a deep breath and relax, letting all of the tightness and tenseness leave. My breathing will now be normal and relaxed, and I will relax the muscles of my stomach. Now I will relax all of the muscles up and down both sides of the spine and let that relaxation spread throughout my back. Now I will relax the waist, buttocks, and thighs down to my knees. Now the relaxation will spread to the calves of my legs, ankles, feet, and toes. I will just stay here and continue to let all of my muscles go completely limp. I will become completely relaxed from the top of my head to the tips of my toes."

If you try this one or two times, you will be amazed at just how relaxed you can become. If you have trouble doing this at first, you might deliberately tense the muscles of various parts of your body a few times and then let them relax completely immediately following the forced tension. This will teach you to discriminate clearly between the tensed and relaxed states and train you to produce relaxation at will. Go through each of the muscle groups just

Go through each of the muscle groups and learn to tense and relax them one by one.

mentioned (forehead and scalp, face, neck, shoulders, etc.) and learn to tense and relax them one by one. You may spend one or two sessions learning to relax just the muscles that are hard for you to relax. Then go through the whole procedure in one sitting. You will find yourself very relaxed at this point.

Do this as an exercise, just the way you would do a physical exercise if you wanted to get in top physical shape. You should do it three or four times a day, every day. Once at midmorning, once at noon, once in the evening, and once at bedtime are the best occasions. Go through the process of relaxing all the muscles, and then stay relaxed for 3 to 5 minutes. After that, you can get up and go about your business.

You will find that you are much more relaxed and calm following the exercise. It should take you only 5 minutes each time for a total of 15 to 20 minutes per day. The payoff—reduced anxiety, which leads to a happier and longer life—is well worth the effort.

Some people find it difficult to find time to do the exercise. If your job allows coffee breaks, that is a good time. You will still have time for your coffee afterward. Of course, too much coffee can make you tense, so you might want to use the entire time for relaxation and skip the cup of coffee—or simply drink decaf. If you don't have coffee breaks, you can go to the rest room at an appropriate time and go through the procedure there (all jobs have a provision for going to the rest room). Also, if you work in a busy place, the rest room may be the best place to do the exercise. Usually it is quieter there, and more privacy is afforded.

Use of this procedure interrupts the feedback loop that is causing the anxiety to spiral. The spiral effect ceases, allowing the anxiety to dissipate. Instead of steadily increasing anxiety until you are in misery by the end of the day, you return periodically to a calm, resting state and start over. At the end of the day you are much more relaxed and less fatigued.

The above exercise can also be used before some type of recreational activity. For example, you can sit down and go through the exercise just before reading a book or watching a television program. You will then find yourself very relaxed and more able to enjoy the recreation. Another useful variation is to perform the exercise and then allow yourself to drift off into a nap. You will awaken very relaxed and refreshed.

This also is an excellent technique to combat insomnia. To use it for insomnia, get in bed and go through the procedure as indicated. After you are fully relaxed, slowly think the word *sleep,* over and over. Generally, I teach this to a patient in my office. The next time the patient returns for an appointment, I'll ask how it went. The answer is often, "It worked very well. In fact, after the first time or two, I never got to the end. I fell asleep in the middle." If you do get through the relaxation process and are still awake, it is important to repeat the word *sleep* (or *relax and sleep*) over and over in your mind. This keeps you from thinking about the concerns of the day or the ones you will face tomorrow. When we think of those things, adrenalin is secreted into the blood stream, activating us and keeping us awake. The old folk remedy of counting sheep is based on this concept of keeping the mind occupied on something boring so that other thoughts that would activate us are kept out of mind.

Once you have learned to relax using this procedure, you may be able to get into the completely relaxed state in a matter of seconds, without going through each set of muscles from head to toe. You will need only to sit or lie in a comfortable position, take a deep breath, exhale, and let all your muscles go limp. The relaxation will be almost instantaneous. This is obviously an ability worth cultivating. It does take diligent, systematic effort, however, just as does developing a muscular physique.

For those who have trouble learning to relax, it is possible to see a professional therapist who can help by using biofeedback. Such training is often well worth the time and expense. Some people like to make these relaxation exercises more interesting by using techniques of meditation along with the relaxation. There are numerous approaches to meditation, most of which derive from Eastern philosophy and religion. Scientific research with

Meditation is emotionally a very rewarding experience leading to deeper insight into yourself and your surroundings.

these techniques has indicated that they do in fact affect bodily and mental processes beneficially when practiced correctly. People who practice them are able to achieve a considerable degree of bodily relaxation and mental calmness. They also report that meditation is emotionally a very rewarding experience leading to deeper insight into themselves and their surroundings.

If you want to try these techniques, you must first get in the right position (the lotus position is the most common one). Sit on the floor and cross your legs so that your right foot rests on your left thigh and your left foot rests on your right thigh. Next, make your back into a straight column, resting on the base of your legs and buttocks, so that it is comfortable and requires no strain to keep the back straight. If you put a pillow under your buttocks, this usually will give you a firm, comfortable base. Keep your head and neck comfortably erect. Rest your hands in your lap. The eyes may be kept open and focused at a point a few feet in front of the body, or they may be closed. This position is rather difficult for many people to assume; if this is the case for you, get as close to the position as you comfortably can and then gently stretch the muscles each time you do the exercise. Eventually you may be able to do it. If not, an alternative is generally referred to as the tailor position. For this one, sit with your buttocks on a cushion and fold the legs in front of you so that the right foot is under the left knee and the left foot is under the right knee. Still another possibility is to sit in a straight-backed chair, with your feet firmly on the floor, back and head erect, and hands in your lap. Choose the position that best fits your anatomy and physical condition. It is important that you be comfortable. Once in position, sway back and forth awhile to get completely comfortable. Then take a few deep breaths. With each breath, let go a little and allow your muscles to relax. Mentally you should begin to clear your mind of the business and rushing that characterize our lives. Begin to adopt a passive, detached attitude of observation. Do not try to achieve a certain state or guide your thinking; just let the attitude grow.

Having done this, you are ready for specific meditation exercises. One Taoist exercise directs the person to concentrate attention on the center of the torso at about the level of the navel. Thoughts, as they arise, should be placed at this level of the body and consciousness should be shifted to the solar plexus (an area in the pit of the stomach where numerous nerves and blood vessels meet). Thoughts take on a different meaning, and one develops a different awareness when things are experienced in this manner. This particular exercise has been the occasion for considerable ridicule about people who sit and contemplate their navels, but if practiced correctly it is a stimulating experience for many.

One Taoist exercise directs the person to concentrate attention on the center of the torso at about the level of the navel.

Another exercise is to concentrate on the feelings and sensations of your existence as a being. Or, you can observe the process of your mind at work in thought. Watch your thoughts develop, feel them, and see how they are formed. Sometimes you may want to take an object and see it as an existence equivalent to yourself. You may want to meditate on a particular person who may be physically present with you or not. You may sometimes want to take a significant object from your past with pleasant connotations and meditate on it—an old photograph, a school paper, a flower from your scrapbook, or some similar object. Some people find it very pleasant to take a fantasy trip while meditating. If you want to do this, think about a place you have been that you liked a great deal. Re-experience it. Transport yourself mentally to the spot. See what is going on. You can concentrate either on seeing it exactly as it was when you were there or on the way you imagine it would be now. You can concentrate on the scenery such as forests, mountains, and lakes, or on the people. Visualize the people in the place one by one and meditate on them. You can meditate, in similar fashion, about a place you would like to visit someday. You can mentally transport yourself to the place and experience it in perhaps an even deeper way than you would if you were actually there. Later, going to the place will be more rewarding than it otherwise would have been. If you have a photograph or a painting, it can be used as part of this exercise.

Another exercise is to concentrate on the feelings and sensations of your existence as a being.

Another interesting exercise is to establish a pattern of slow, deep breathing. After you have established this pattern, think of the number *1* as you exhale. Then take a breath and think of the number *2*. Do this until you have reached 10 or 15. A variation that you can try later is to mentally place the numbers beside and on top of one another in your stomach as you exhale. Keep them there and note how you feel once the mind has shifted to the center of your body. This is a classic Zen technique.

You may find meditating to a certain sound interesting. One way to do this is to listen to some music you like. Experience it, feel it, go with it wherever it takes you. You may want to let your body move with the music. This is often an exhilarating experience. Many people like to chant during their meditation. A *mantra* is a sacred sound that, in some forms of Buddhism, is passed from the master to a disciple. In India the greatest mantra is *om*. It is said to represent God in all his fullness. To use this chant, think of *om* as though it were divided into three separate syllables of equal length. Take a deep breath, and as you exhale, make the sound *owww* as in *cow*, then slide into *ooou* as in *blue*, and then into *mmmm*. Take another breath and do it again. Do this for a few minutes. Some people liken the effect to an internal massage. They also report calmness and expanded consciousness following.

You may, of course, use other standard chants or develop your own. Many people like to pray during their meditative exercises. Prayers should be focused on one simple idea or a short passage from a religious writing. Think about what this means and how it can apply to your life. In meditation one can develop a deeper inner communication with and a sense of the presence of God. Others find meditating on a poem or a line from a poem rewarding; a passage from a book can serve the same purpose.

Many Eastern and Western writers who meditate have written of their reflections and experiences. These can be very useful as material for meditation and reflection. You may want to meditate on a koan (kō-ŏn). A *koan* is a seemingly nonsensical question that serves as a stimulus and focus for meditation. The word *koan* means literally a public document or a statement, but also refers

A koan is a seemingly nonsensical question that serves as a stimulus and focus for meditation.

to a declaration that a master makes to a disciple for the disciple's instruction. There are many right answers to a koan, and yet there is no answer. The koan makes us aware of the limits of words and the depths of mind and existence. For example, one that has had considerable popularity in this country is "You have heard the sound of two hands when they clap together. What is the sound of one hand clapping? What is this sound for one thousand?" Other such koans are: "Show me your face before your father and mother were born," or, "Where do we meet after you are dead, cremated, and the ashes are scattered around?" Another is "All things are said to return to One. Where, then, is the ultimate home of this One?"

Sometimes the koan takes the form of a paradoxical command, as in, "Use your spade, which is in your empty hands," or, "Walk while riding a donkey." Many times they take the form of seemingly nonsensical answers to questions. "Who is Buddha?" Answer: "Three pounds of flax"; or, "What is the essence of Buddhism?" Answer: "My, what a large melon this is." One famous koan was for the master to hold up his walking stick in front of his disciples and say, "This is not a stick. What do you call it?"

Most of the exercises that have been discussed here are best performed for half an hour to an hour on a daily basis, unless otherwise indicated. It is not necessary to do them every day, but disciplined, regular use of them brings the best results. Beginners should not make the sessions too long.

For those interested in meditation, more information may be found in the public library or bookstores. The interested person may want to look into Zen, Yoga, transcendental meditation, T'ai Chi, and similar areas. One of the better basic books for beginners is *The Three Pillars of Zen* by Philip Kapleau, but there are many other excellent books available.

A word of caution is in order. Many people find meditation exercises beneficial if practiced properly, but others may find them upsetting. If you feel that they would be upsetting, don't do them. For those who do these exercises, it is best to start gradually and go only as far as you can with comfort. It is also best to work with

Differential relaxation *means that some muscle groups can be relaxed while the others work.*

If you learn to practice differential relaxation, you will see a general reduction of your tension and anxiety level, leaving you with a lot more energy and vitality at the end of the day.

and be supervised by someone with training and experience in this area.

One final relaxation exercise is sometimes referred to as *differential relaxation*. It is easy to understand and can be employed readily with a little practice. The basic point is that when we are sitting, standing, walking, running, or whatever, some muscle groups can be relaxed while the others work. We tend to tense and work many muscles throughout the day that could be in a state of relaxation. We do this because we typically involve our whole selves in what we are doing; sometimes, though, we may be overdoing it. It is obvious that while sitting, many muscles can be relaxed. But even while running or walking, the arms, shoulders, back, and facial muscles, for example, can also be relaxed.

Analyze your daily activities and see how much relaxation can be worked in. Then discipline yourself to keep muscles relaxed rather than tensed when possible. Disciplining yourself is the difficult part. You will keep forgetting. One way to remind yourself is to paint a small red dot on the crystal of your watch. Then every time you look at your watch, you will be reminded to check for any muscles that can be relaxed while you are doing what you are doing.

If you learn to practice differential relaxation, you will see a general reduction of your tension and anxiety level, leaving you with a lot more energy and vitality at the end of the day. One physician, Edmund Jacobson, wrote extensively on the use of this and other relaxation procedures for the reduction of anxiety. He found them very successful with patients who were tense. A couple of his more helpful books are *Anxiety and Tension Control: A Physiologic Approach* and *You Must Relax: A Practical Method of Reducing the Strains of Modern Living.* Another physician, Herbert Benson, has written two very helpful books in this area, *The Relaxation Response* (with Miriam Z. Klipper) and *Beyond the Relaxation Response* (with William Proctor). Benson stresses the benefits of learning to relax for good physical health.

Remember, if you want to develop physical strength, physical exercise is the way to do it. If you want to relax and reduce anxiety, the relaxation exercises outlined in this chapter can help you achieve that goal. (For more information on adding the benefits of physical exercise to your relaxation exercises, see Chapter 10.)

STRESS MANAGEMENT EXERCISES

1. To better understand the role of stress in your life, keep a daily journal (outlined below) for the coming week. You may make additional copies of this form for future use. Use a scale of 1 to 100 for your ratings.

Day 1. highest level of stress today = _____
lowest level of stress today = _____
average level of stress today = _____

The main source of my stress today was . . .

_____

_____

_____

_____

_____

_____

_____

_____

_____

In order to handle this better, I must . . .

_____

_____

_____

_____

_____

_____

_____

_____

_____

_____

_____

_____

_____

_____

Day 2. highest level of stress today = _____

lowest level of stress today = _____

average level of stress today = _____

The main source of my stress today was . . .

_____

_____

_____

_____

_____

_____

_____

_____

_____

_____

In order to handle this better, I must . . .

_____

_____

_____

_____

_____

_____

_____

_____

_____

_____

_____

_____

Day 3. highest level of stress today = _____
         lowest level of stress today = _____
         average level of stress today = _____

The main source of my stress today was . . .

_____

_____

_____

_____

_____

_____

_____

_____

_____

_____

In order to handle this better, I must . . .

_____

_____

_____

_____

_____

_____

_____

_____

_____

_____

_____

_____

_____

_____

Day 4. highest level of stress today = _____
        lowest level of stress today = _____
        average level of stress today = _____

The main source of my stress today was . . .

_____

_____

_____

_____

_____

_____

_____

_____

In order to handle this better, I must . . .

_____

_____

_____

_____

_____

_____

_____

_____

_____

_____

_____

_____

_____

Day 5. highest level of stress today = _____
lowest level of stress today = _____
average level of stress today = _____

The main source of my stress today was . . .

_____

_____

_____

_____

_____

_____

_____

_____

_____

In order to handle this better, I must . . .

_____

_____

_____

_____

_____

_____

_____

_____

_____

_____

_____

_____

Day 6. highest level of stress today = _____

lowest level of stress today = _____

average level of stress today = _____

The main source of my stress today was . . .

_____

_____

_____

_____

_____

_____

_____

In order to handle this better, I must . . .

_____

_____

_____

_____

_____

_____

_____

_____

_____

_____

_____

_____

Day 7.   highest level of stress today = _____
          lowest level of stress today = _____
          average level of stress today = _____

The main source of my stress today was . . .

_____

_____

_____

_____

_____

_____

_____

_____

_____

In order to handle this better, I must . . .

_____

_____

_____

_____

_____

_____

_____

_____

_____

_____

_____

_____

_____

2. Relaxation is the basis for many of the approaches available for stress management. In this exercise you will practice some basic relaxation techniques and develop skill in this area. First, read the following script:

To begin, relax all of the muscles in the scalp. Let all of the tension and pressure go out of those muscles and let them relax completely. Simply tell those muscles to relax. Now, move down to the forehead. Smooth the muscles of the forehead and make them relax. Then, move to the face and tell all of the muscles of the cheeks and jaw to relax. Let the jaw drop slightly. Relax all of the muscles of the head. Now, relax the muscles of the neck. Let all of the pressure go out of these muscles and let them relax. Move down to your shoulders and let all of the tension go out of these muscles. Let your shoulders sag and relax. Move down the arms to the elbows, relaxing all of those muscles. Then, move to the forearms, the wrists, the hands and fingers, relaxing all of these muscles. Just let your arms dangle from the frame of your body. Now, relax the muscles of the chest. Take a deep breath and as you exhale, let all of the muscles of the chest relax. Let all of the pressure and tension go out of these muscles. Then let this proceed down to the stomach. Let all of those muscles relax and become calm. Now, go up and down the spine, relaxing all of the small muscles up and down the spine. Then, let the relaxation radiate throughout the rest of the back, relaxing all of the muscles and letting them be calm. Now, relax all of the muscles of the waist, buttocks, and thighs. Let these muscles relax completely and let all of the pressure go out. Move down to the knees, relaxing them and letting them become calm. Move down to the calves of your legs, to the ankles, feet, and toes. Relax. Just let all of the pressure go out of your whole body. Let every muscle relax and become completely calm . . . perfectly relaxed from the top of your head to the tip of your toes. Take a deep breath and as you exhale, let all of the pressure and tension go out of your body. Let every muscle relax and let a wave of calm go through your body. Take another breath and let all of the pressure and tension go out of your body as you exhale. Say to yourself, "I am peaceful. I am calm."

If a particular part of your body is not completely relaxed, concentrate on that part and repeat the relaxation instructions for the area that is not relaxed. You can do this exercise alone but it works better with a partner. If you have a partner, take turns reading the previous instructions to each other and relaxing. If you do the exercise alone, you may just read the instructions to yourself while relaxing or you may make an audio tape to play so that you can concentrate on relaxing rather than reading. Rate yourself on a scale of 0 to 100 with respect to how relaxed you are as you begin this exercise.

Before relaxation exercise rating = _____.

When you are finished with the exercise, rate your degree of relaxation.

After relaxation exercise rating = _____. Write a brief paragraph on your thoughts and reactions to this exercise in the space below:

_____
_____
_____
_____
_____
_____
_____
_____
_____
_____
_____
_____
_____
_____
_____
_____
_____
_____

3. Repeat the process outlined in Item 2, interspersing instructions to first tense each muscle set before relaxing the muscles. For example:

First, tense all of the muscles in your forehead and scalp. Make all of the muscles in the scalp tight and tense. Wrinkle your forehead and create pressure in those muscles. Now, relax all of the muscles in the scalp. Let all of the pressure go out of those muscles and let them relax completely. Simply tell those muscles to relax. Now, move down to the forehead. Smooth the muscles of the forehead and make them relax. Now tense the muscles of the face and cheeks and clench the jaws. Feel the pressure. Then, tell all of the muscles of the face, cheeks and jaw to relax . . . etc.

Repeat the procedure for any body parts that are not totally relaxed. Do this alone or take turns with your partner as before. Rate your relaxation (on a scale of 0 to 100).

Before tense/relaxation exercise _____.
After tense/relaxation exercise _____.

4. Briefly compare the two relaxation exercises. Which worked better for you?

_____

_____

_____

_____

_____

_____

_____

_____

_____

_____

_____

_____

_____

_____

_____

_____

5. Now, choose a location where you can be alone and undisturbed to do the rest of this exercise on your own. First, get in a comfortable position. Read the relaxation instructions to yourself, and after you have reached a state of relaxation, repeat three times a phrase that you believe will help you relax further, such as, "I am peaceful. I am calm." Then, think of a very peaceful scene such as a quiet lake or a meadow or similar place. Use this imagery to further relax. After a few minutes, open your eyes.

Rate your relaxation on a scale of 0 to 100.

Before this exercise _____.
After this exercise _____.

6. Write your thoughts comparing the three relaxation exercises, and decide which is best for you.

_____

_____

_____

_____

_____

_____

_____

_____

_____

_____

_____

_____

_____

_____

_____

_____

_____

7. Breathing is significantly influenced by our level of stress. Shallow breathing (chest breathing) is associated with high levels of stress. Deep breathing (abdomen breathing) tends to be associated with lower levels of stress. It is sometimes possible to reduce stress by changing from shallow to deep breathing. Practice the following exercises to become adept at deep breathing.

First, stretch out on the floor or sit in your chair. Next, place one hand on your abdomen, right above the waistline, and the other hand in the middle of your chest. Breathe normally and determine by touch and by observing the movement of your hands whether you are more of a shallow or a deep breather. If you're a shallow breather, the hand on your chest will move more and you will feel it more there. If you're a deep breather, you will notice the same in the hand on your abdomen. Write about which type of breather you are.

_____

_____

_____

_____

_____

_____

_____

_____

_____

_____

_____

_____

_____

_____

_____

_____

_____

_____

_____

8. Now, practice deep breathing. Before you begin, rate your degree of relaxation on the scale at the end of this paragraph. Then, consciously lower your diaphragm and your abdomen while breathing through your nose. Take a deep breath in this manner, hold it for a second or two and slowly exhale through your nose. Repeat this three more times. Rate your degree of relaxation on a scale of 0 to 100.

Before the breathing exercise _____.

After the breathing exercise _____.

This effect can be further enhanced by lifting the shoulders and/or moving the arms slightly away from the body while taking a breath. Practice deep breathing in a series of three to five breaths several times per day. With time, you can train yourself to be a deep breather. When you find that your stress level is increasing during the day, take one very deep breath enhanced by raising your shoulders and moving the arms slightly away from your body. Hold the breath for a second or two and sigh as you exhale. This will immediately reduce your stress level slightly.

9. In the space below compare the breathing exercise with the other relaxation exercises. Which worked best for you?

_____

_____

_____

_____

_____

_____

_____

_____

_____

_____

_____

_____

_____

_____

_____

10. Numerous relaxation and meditation exercises can lead to better self-understanding. You may find the following exercise on focusing interesting. *Focusing* is a technique to help one identify and correctly label feelings. Try this technique using the following instructions. If at any time you become uncomfortable with any of these exercises, simply stop the process and open your eyes. The lack of structure in some of these exercises can be upsetting to some people. If they are upsetting, they should be terminated.

Get in a comfortable position. Close your eyes and do a brief relaxation exercise. You may use one that you have learned previously or you may simply take three deep breaths, relaxing all of your muscles as you exhale.

Mentally go to the place in your body where you usually experience a physical sensation associated with stress. This may be in the gut, chest, head, neck, shoulders, back, or any other area. Concentrate on that area and recall the physical sensations that you generally experience in this area when you are under stress.

Now, concentrate on the feeling or emotion that you generally have with that physical sensation during times of stress.

As you concentrate on the feeling, ask yourself what that feeling is saying to you in *words*. That is, what is the meaning of that feeling? When you have completed this task, open your eyes and answer the questions in Items 11 through 14.

11. What area of your body did you select as the one where you generally experience stress?

_____

_____

_____

_____

_____

_____

_____

_____

12. Describe the physical sensation you generally have (e.g. butterflies, headache, muscle cramp, etc.).

_____

_____

_____

_____

_____

_____

_____

_____

_____

_____

_____

_____

13. How would you describe the feeling or emotion you generally experience?

_____

_____

_____

_____

_____

_____

_____

_____

_____

_____

14. What words or meanings came to you as you attempted to label the feeling?

_____

_____

_____

_____

_____

_____

_____

_____

_____

_____

_____

_____

_____

15. On a scale of 0 to 100 (0 = totally comfortable and 100 = very uncomfortable), how comfortable were you during this exercise?

   Rating = _____.

16. Choose one of the meditation techniques discussed in this chapter and try it, writing your experience and thoughts about this exercise in the following space. Try some of the others, if you wish, and compare them.

_____

_____

_____

_____

_____

_____

_____

_____

7

Systematic Desensitization

MANY OF THE ANXIETIES that people experience are due to
what psychologists call *conditioned reactions.* Simply stated, this
term means that things that frequently occur together in our experience become linked or associated with one another so that we
respond to them in the same, or a highly similar, way when they
happen again. Thus, if we are made anxious or afraid in the presence of certain factors (psychologists refer to them as stimuli),
these same factors or stimuli will make us anxious when they occur later, even if the situation in reality no longer poses an actual
threat. For example, you may have had a number of experiences
as a child in which a person in authority, such as a school princi-
pal, police officer, or guard, frightened and perhaps punished you
in some way. Your reaction as an adult to someone in authority
may produce considerably more anxiety than the situation really
calls for because of the previous conditioning of strong anxiety to
people in that position.

A person thus conditioned might be driving along a highway
obeying all traffic laws and in the rearview mirror see a police car
pull up. The person may feel considerable anxiety at the approach
of the car. If the police officer stops the person, he or she may have

*Things that frequently
occur together in our
experience become
linked or associated with
one another so that we
respond to them in the
same, or a highly
similar, way when they
happen again—that is,
we have a* conditioned
reaction.

many symptoms of anxiety such as a pounding heart, rapid breathing, muscular tenseness, and stuttering/stammering speech. This is an overreaction to the situation; the person was breaking no law, and the officer may only want to tell him or her that a taillight is broken or warn of a road hazard ahead. At worst, the driver may have broken a minor traffic law, which would cost a fine of a few dollars. For many, however, the situation evokes anxiety near panic. Such effects often result from conditioned reactions.

Many of our emotions seem to be based largely on such responses. Conditioned reactions are somewhat similar to reflexes, but they are learned rather than inherited. Their automatic or reflexive character, however, explains why it is hard to discuss things rationally with someone who is emotionally involved in a situation—such a person is responding more through conditioned reactions to the present stimuli than relating to the realities of the situation. It also explains why we can tell ourselves that the next time a situation occurs we are not going to let it upset us and are going to handle it a certain way, only to find that when it does occur, we respond pretty much as we always have. This is the nature of conditioned reactions.

Now, if many of our anxieties are conditioned reactions, what can we do about them? Are we the victims of our traumatic pasts, or can we overcome such anxieties? Fortunately, we can overcome them. In fact, they are amazingly *easy* to overcome if we work at them in the right way. For decades psychologists have studied conditioned reactions in laboratories all over the world. A clinical procedure for eliminating conditioned anxiety reactions, developed by psychiatrist Joseph Wolpe, makes use of the basic principles learned from this research. The procedure is called *systematic desensitization,* and if done properly, it works almost every time.

Let's use an example to show how you can use systematic desensitization on your own. Suppose authority figures are your problem. The first step would be to sit down with some index cards and on each card write a different situation or experience that causes you anxiety in this area. After you have a stack of cards,

One clinical procedure for eliminating conditioned anxiety reactions is systematic desensitization.

place them in order, with the one that causes the least anxiety on top and the one that causes the most anxiety on the bottom. Your list might look something like this (least anxiety-causing at the top, most anxiety-causing at the bottom):

Sit down with some index cards and on each card write a different situation or experience that causes you anxiety.

1. Walking past and greeting one of the bosses at work who is only a little older than I.

2. Walking past and greeting one of the bosses at work who is considerably older than I—one with gray hair and a gruff but somewhat pleasant demeanor.

3. Encountering one of the bosses who is only a little older than I in the coffee-break room, where we will have to talk and have coffee together.

4. Encountering one of the bosses who is considerably older than I—with gray hair and a gruff but somewhat pleasant demeanor—in the coffee-break room, where we will have to talk and have coffee together.

5. Having one of the bosses who is only a little older than I watch me, without seeming pleased or displeased, while I work.

6. Having one of the bosses who is considerably older than I—with gray hair and a gruff but somewhat pleasant demeanor—watch me while I work, without seeming pleased or displeased.

7. Having one of the bosses who is only a little older than I watch me while I work and seeming to be displeased with what I am doing.

8. Having one of the bosses who is considerably older than I—with gray hair and a gruff but somewhat pleasant demeanor—watch me while I work and seem to be displeased with what I am doing.

9. Having one of the bosses who is only a little older than I watch me while I work and make a slightly critical comment to me after watching for a while.

10. Having one of the bosses who is considerably older than I—with gray hair and a gruff but somewhat pleasant demeanor—watch me while I work and make a slightly critical comment to me after watching for a while.

11. Having one of the bosses who is only a little older than I watch me while I work and make a very critical comment after watching for a while.

12. Having one of the bosses who is considerably older than I—with gray hair and a gruff but somewhat pleasant demeanor—watch me while I work and make a very critical comment after watching for a while.

13. Attending a conference in the office of one of the bosses who is only a little older than I to discuss something about my work that should be improved.

14. Attending a conference in the office of one of the bosses who is considerably older than I—with gray hair and a gruff but somewhat pleasant demeanor—to discuss something about my work that should be improved.

15. Attending a conference with several bosses both young and old to discuss something about my work that should be improved.

Note that in this example we have varied several stimuli having to do with age, demeanor, intensity of contact, and degree of criticism, but the items are still rank-ordered by the amount of anxiety they would likely produce.

The next step in systematic desensitization is to relax completely.

The next step in systematic desensitization is to relax completely. You can do this by using the procedures learned in the previous chapter. First sit in a comfortable chair or lie on a couch or bed. Then say something like the following to yourself: "I am going to relax completely. I will relax my forehead and scalp. I will let all the muscles of my forehead and scalp relax and become completely at rest. All of the wrinkles will smooth out of my forehead and that part of my body will relax completely. Now I will relax the muscles of my face. I will just let them relax and go limp. There will be no tension in my jaw. Next I will relax my neck muscles. Just let them become tranquil and allow all of the pressure to leave them. My neck muscles are relaxing completely. Now I will relax the muscles of my shoulders. That relaxation will spread down my arms to the elbows, down the forearms to my wrists, hands, and fingers. My arms will just dangle from the frame of my body. I will now relax the muscles of my chest. I will let them relax. I will take a deep breath and relax, letting all of the tightness and tenseness leave. My breathing will now be normal and relaxed, and I will relax the muscles of my stomach. Now I will relax all of the muscles up and down both sides of the spine and let that relaxation spread throughout my back. Now I will relax the waist, buttocks, and thighs down to my knees. Now the relaxation will spread to the calves of my legs, ankles, feet, and toes. I will just lie here and continue to let all of my muscles go completely limp. I will become completely relaxed from the top of my head to the tips of my toes."

If you try this one or two times, you will be amazed at just how relaxed you can become. If you have trouble doing this at first, you might try purposely tensing the muscles of various parts of your body a few times and then letting them relax completely immediately following the forced tension. As discussed in the previous chapter, this will teach you to discriminate clearly between the tense and relaxed states and train you in producing relaxation at will. Go through each of the muscle groups mentioned above (forehead and scalp, face, neck, shoulders, etc.) and learn to relax them one by one.

After you are completely relaxed, you are ready to begin the systematic desensitization. Take the top card from the pile and look at it. Then close your eyes and visualize the situation described on it as vividly as you can in your imagination. Imagine it occurring and imagine that you are really there. As you do that, you may experience some anxiety. If so, stop the imaginary scene at once and go back to relaxing all of your muscles. In general, taking just a deep breath or two and letting all of the muscles rest will do the job. If you need to, however, go through the whole relaxation sequence in your mind again, muscle by muscle.

When you are again completely relaxed, wait a few seconds. Then look at the card and imagine the scene once more. If you feel anxiety, make your mind turn blank, stop imagining the scene, and go back to relaxing. Do this over and over until you can imagine the scene without feeling anxiety. It may take only once or twice or it may take 15 to 20 times, but repeat it until you can imagine the scene without feeling anxiety. When you have accomplished this, go on to the second scene. Continue in this manner until you have gone through all the cards.

It is best to work on the scenes like this for about half an hour at a time. You may want to do it every day or every other day, or only a couple of times a week, depending on your schedule and how quickly you want to conquer the anxiety. Usually, from one session to the next, it is a good idea to start by going over the last item or two that you were able to imagine without anxiety from the previous session.

A variation of the above procedure is to tape record a vivid description of the scene in advance. Then relax and listen to the tape. If you feel anxious, shut the tape off and relax. When calm, rewind the tape and begin again.

When you have completed this process for one of the scenes on a card, you will find that this situation—the thought of which used to cause stabbing pains of anxiety—can now be thought of calmly, without disturbance. You have been desensitized. To make the treatment complete, you should now calmly go over in your mind what is the right thing to do in that situation and actually make plans to do the right thing the next time the situation occurs. You will be amazed to find that your previous anxiety kept you so tense that you avoided thinking or planning in this area, and that it prevented clear thinking when you were in the situation. This will all be different now.

It is a good idea, as you desensitize yourself to each of the scenes on the cards, to plan how to handle that situation and then seek out several occasions when you can practice handling it. Some people go through the relaxation procedure just before confronting the real situation; others just take a deep breath and get as relaxed and composed as they can. Many of my patients have been so elated by the effects of this treatment that they have deliberately sought out situations that previously caused them great anxiety, frustration, and failure. Once you have desensitized yourself to the situations and experienced them a few times in real life, you will find that they are actually conquered and cause you no discomfort at all. It may seem almost too good to be true, but it does work.

If you have trouble going through the procedure alone, you might want to enlist the help of a friend. Often you can arrange to trade roles and desensitize each other. If you do this, have the friend instruct you step by step to relax all of your muscles and then describe the scene vividly to you while you stay relaxed. You will need to tell the friend enough details about the scene so that he or she can weave an imaginary story, one you can really put yourself into and experience. If you feel anxiety at any time, signal the friend by raising the index finger of your right hand. The friend should, at that instant, tell you to turn off your imagination, make your mind go blank, and return to relaxing. When you are relaxed, the process can begin again.

Another way of handling conditioned anxiety that works just as well as the preceding method in most cases—and better in some—is called *in vivo desensitization*. The term *in vivo* here simply means "in real life." To do this you again make a list of situations and arrange them in order, as described before. This time, however, skip the imagination part and simply plan in advance how to handle each situation. Then seek out the least anxiety-provoking situation, relax, and carry out your plan. Analyze the results after each try and figure out better ways to respond to and handle the situation the next time; then do it again. Repeat this process until you conquer one item on the list, then go on to the next and the

It is a good idea, as you desensitize yourself to each of the scenes on the cards, to plan how to handle that situation and then seek out several occasions when you can practice handling it.

In in vivo desensitization, we skip the imagination part and simply plan in advance how to handle each situation.

next until you are comfortable with each and can handle all of them. Remember that "those who would move mountains must start with the pebbles at the foot of the hill."

For an example of in vivo desensitization, suppose you have a lot of anxiety in social situations. After thinking about the problem you might develop a hierarchy that looks like this (least anxiety-causing at top, most at bottom).

1. Making small talk with a stranger at a bus stop.

2. Having a fairly extended conversation with a stranger in the doctor's waiting room or similar place.

3. Running into a friend on the street and being introduced by that friend to the person with him or her, and talking briefly with the new person.

4. Meeting a new person at a party and having to make conversation for a few minutes.

5. Meeting several new people at a party and making small talk.

6. Meeting a new person who joins you and some mutual friends for dinner.

7. Meeting several new people who join you and some mutual friends for dinner.

8. Being the only new person at a dinner party who must meet several people for the first time, sit at a table of strangers, and have dinner with them.

The way to attack the problem in this case would be to take the first item and look for naturally occurring occasions—or even arrange for occasions to occur—in which you can experience the event. You should prepare for the occasion in a way that is logical and appropriate. Being prepared is half the battle; in this case, you might make a point of reading the newspaper to glean some topics to talk about. You might go over mentally various pleasantries that seem to contribute to a congenial encounter. You might keep an appropriate joke or anecdote in the back of your mind, or you might search the interests of the person you meet for something you have in common. A compliment on how a person looks or on something interesting he or she said will seldom lead you astray and will often make a friend for life. The point is, plan in advance how you will handle the occasion. Then when the occasion arises, work out what you have planned.

As a boy, I used to work on a truck farm. The foreman had a large sign on the blackboard at the barn that read, "Plan the work and work the plan." It's good advice. Just before you enter the situation, go through the relaxation procedure or at least take a few deep breaths, shrug your shoulders, and get completely relaxed. Then go in and do the best you can. After it's over, think about and analyze how things went. Learn from each experience how to perform better next time. Then do it again. Eventually the anxiety will be gone and you will have developed a repertoire of skills to handle such situations. At that point, you will no longer need the elaborate plans. Your skills will just come naturally. Be sure to start with the least anxiety-provoking situation. Go on to the next highest and the next only after the ones before it have been conquered. Success depends on a careful, systematic attack.

Success depends on a careful, systematic attack.

The previous example deals with social situations involving strangers. Obviously you could devise similar hierarchies involving friends or involving different types of socialization (e.g., job interviews or public speaking) or a variety of other uncomfortable situations. Most people have been conditioned to react with anxiety to enough situations that they may devise hierarchies in several different areas and work through them. If you have more than one hierarchy at a time that you want to work on, you can work a little on each in every session or go through one completely in a series of sessions before beginning the next.

Some people have used an approach between the imagination and in vivo approaches we've discussed. This approach is called *behavioral rehearsal,* and in it, you rehearse with a friend things that you would like to do without anxiety. For example, for a job in-

Behavioral rehearsal *is simply rehearsing with a friend things that you would like to do without anxiety.*

terview, have a friend play the part of the interviewer. The friend can play the parts of different kinds of interviewers (stern, hostile, friendly, etc.), and you can practice being calm and responding to the questions. At the end, you can discuss how you might have better handled the situation. Then try it again. Do it over and over until you act without anxiety. The different types of interviews and interviewers can be arranged in hierarchies and worked through using this method.

The hardest part of using these procedures is developing the hierarchies. Often the root of anxiety is vague—hard to define or separate out from other factors. The basic strategy in doing so is to keep the scenes as simple and straightforward as possible. The best way to start is simply to write down on cards as many situations that involve anxiety as possible without worrying about categories or hierarchies. After you have done that, sort them out into logical categories involving one dimension or a couple of dimensions that seem to go together well. Each of these piles will become a hierarchy of its own. Read over all the items in a given pile and fill in the gaps by writing new cards that obviously would fit in with the ones already written. Extend the range upward and downward by making up more (or less) extreme situations. Eventually you will develop a hierarchy with 10 to 25 items. If you have more than 25 or so, break your hierarchy into two or more hierarchies.

It's common to wonder if you are including the right things in your hierarchies. The best way to answer this question is to make each scene as specific and as close to real life as you can. If a scene is a specific, real-life situation that makes you anxious, it is right for the hierarchy.

If you have trouble staying relaxed and getting past the first item on the hierarchy, you have started out with one that is too threatening. Write some less anxiety-provoking items, and extend your list downward. If you reach a point at which you have conquered an item but the next one on the list does not seem to be getting any better—after, say, 15 or 20 trials—you probably have made too big a jump. Write some additional items that would logically fit in between the two, and work on them.

An anxiety-producing event that doesn't seem to have a logical hierarchy to go with it is often a very unique event, sometimes one that will happen only once in our lives. For example, your upcoming wedding might be causing anxiety. The way to use the systematic desensitization procedure for such events is to imagine the whole event step by step, from beginning to end, while staying relaxed. At the first sign of anxiety, stop, make your mind turn blank, then go back to the beginning and start over. Keep this up until you can imagine the whole thing without anxiety. You'll find yourself much more relaxed when the event actually occurs than if you had not tried this procedure.

One further tip: Imagination, behavioral rehearsal, and in vivo desensitization all work on essentially the same principle. We generally use the imagination and rehearsal procedures for situations that don't occur often enough in real life to make the in vivo system practical or when the situation is so anxiety-provoking that we are too terrified to try it in real life. In vivo desensitization should be used as often as possible either alone or following the other two methods.

The procedures presented in this chapter work well and can be applied to a large number of anxieties in various areas of life. Since they are based on research findings, they must be done correctly to work. Some people have trouble knowing how to get started or run into difficulties along the way. If this happens, it is best to consult a mental health professional for assistance. Often the therapist will be able to give you some advice on how to handle the problems you are having so that you can continue on your own. Sometimes the therapist may feel that your situation is sufficiently difficult that it would be best for you to see him or her regularly for a period of time to work on the problems under supervision. This is particularly true if you have major panic attacks or suffer from more serious problems, such as agoraphobia (the fear of being in public places from which escape would be difficult or em-

To locate a suitable therapist, call the chair of the psychology or psychiatry department at a nearby university and ask for the names of mental health professionals.

barrassing). These problems are beyond the scope of this book but have been intensively studied in recent years. They can be treated readily by medication and professional psychotherapy. To locate a suitable therapist, call the chair of the psychology or psychiatry department at a nearby university and ask for the names of mental health professionals in your area who practice behavior therapy using systematic desensitization.

STRESS MANAGEMENT EXERCISES

1. Using the behavior rehearsal method outlined in this chapter (see pages 123–126), think of a situation that is coming up in your life that is likely to make you anxious; for example, a meeting with your boss, a job interview, or a similar event. Have a friend play the part of the boss or the interviewer, and practice the event as you anticipate it might happen. Use relaxation techniques to stay calm as you enact the scene. Get feedback from your friend on how you did. Relax and do it over again. Do it over and over until you can do it without discomfort. Then, when the event actually happens, use the relaxation skills you practiced. In the following space, analyze how things went. Were you more relaxed than you thought you would be? Did you do well or not so well? How can you do better next time?

_____

_____

_____

_____

_____

_____

_____

_____

_____

_____

_____

_____

2. Using the methods described on pages 116–121 choose a simple phobia that you would like to work on and follow the directions to do so. You might choose a fear of insects, water, heights, or something of that sort. If you have trouble doing it on your own, try doing it with a friend. Write down your reactions and how things went.

_____

_____

_____

_____

_____

_____

_____

_____

_____

_____

_____

_____

_____

_____

3. Pick another simple phobia and try using the in vivo procedures described on pages 121–123. Discuss your success with this method.

_____

_____

_____

_____

_____

_____

_____

_____

_____

_____

_____

_____

_____

_____

_____

_____

_____

4. In the following space, compare your successes with the previous methods. Which one worked best for you? If you had limited success with these methods, it may be that you need some professional help and guidance to be successful with them. They work well when done properly, but can be a bit tricky for a beginner. Also, if you have a more difficult or complicated phobia or fear you may need professional help. Call the chair of the psychology department at a nearby university and ask for the names of behavioral practitioners in your area who are trained in the use of systematic desensitization. Make an appointment and work on the problem(s) you are concerned about. Then, write a paragraph outlining what you learned from this experience.

_____

_____

_____

_____

_____

_____

_____

_____

_____

_____

_____

8

Assertion

ONE OF THE MOST effective ways to keep anxiety at a minimum in our lives is to deal with problems as they arise, without putting them off. If we put off dealing with a problem, often something that would have been easy to handle grows in seriousness and gets out of hand. Nipping things in the bud is a secret of success that many highly successful people have learned to use. Another problem with procrastination is that even if the situation does not really become worse, our anxiety about it increases until what is actually a minor material problem becomes a major *psychological* hurdle. In our minds it can become a major problem.

If we handle tasks and problems as they come along, it stands to reason that we will have less anxiety in the long run because we will have fewer unsolved problems nagging us. We will also be more able to enjoy our other activities and leisure because we have gotten the problem out of the way. For example, you may have a job to do that would take one hour to complete and would leave the remainder of the day or the evening free for relaxation. If you do the job first and get it out of the way, you can relax completely with a clear conscience; but if you try to relax first, while planning to do the job later, you often will find that you are unable to relax.

One of the most effective ways to keep anxiety at a minimum in our lives is to deal with problems as they arise, without putting them off.

The knowledge that the job is not done yet and that you will have to do it soon keeps you tense.

I once had a patient who told me that life was a clam. At first I thought this was some sort of delusional statement, but when I asked him to explain, he said, "You have to jump on it and pry it open to get the goodies out."

There is an old saying that the best defense is a good offense. While this is not always true, it works in many situations. Psychologists frequently refer to learning to take action in the right way and at the right time as *assertion training*. The idea behind it is that by taking appropriate positive action, we solve problems and prevent the buildup of anxiety.

Fear often results from a feeling of helplessness. Doing something about a problem gives us the feeling of adequacy and success—the antidote for the helpless feelings that often accompany anxiety. Any kind of action usually helps somewhat; appropriate action helps the most. Many athletes and performers know that most of their anxiety occurs before the game or before they get on stage. Once they get into action, the anxiety leaves. Most of us have had this same experience in one way or another. When we face problems head-on, we discover that they were not nearly as bad as we had imagined them to be in our anxious ruminations.

Norman Vincent Peale tells a story about something that happened on his honeymoon, when he and his new wife were alone in a secluded mountain retreat. Peale happened to hear over the radio that a dangerous killer was on the loose in the area. He immediately began to be afraid that they might be in danger. After a while, he heard a sound from the front of their cabin. There were footsteps on the front porch. They stopped in front of the door. Though very frightened, Peale decided he had to do something. With all the courage he could muster, he went to the door and threw it open. There on the porch was a small chipmunk! If we face them head-on, a lot of the killers in our lives turn out to be chipmunks.

Some time ago, my neighbor was taking a trip and asked me to watch his boat while he was gone. Vandals had been stealing motors from boats in the area. One night while he was gone, I looked out the window and saw two men trying to get the motor from my neighbor's boat. Without thinking, I went charging out of the house, pointed a finger at the two, and told them to stop right there. Fortunately they both got up and ran. After they were gone, it dawned on me that I was standing there alone in my pajamas pointing a finger at two men armed with wrenches and hammers. If they had not run, it would not have been much of a contest. The point is that pure, simple assertion will take you a long way. Appropriate assertion is better and will get you farther in the long run.

We will talk more about appropriate assertion in the latter part of this chapter. First, however, it is important to distinguish between assertion and aggression. *Assertion* is attacking a problem, standing up for one's rights, or doing the right thing at the right time. We are simply doing what we believe to be the right thing in the situation and we do it without malice. *Aggression* applies to a situation in which our attack is mixed with hostility and malice. We often realize that we are going too far or are overreacting due to our anger, but we go ahead anyhow. Assertion is a mature, balanced, and fair approach. Aggression, generally, is an immature one that is seldom fair. For example, suppose somebody does something we don't like. The aggressive response might be to confront that person in a heated argument or look for some way to get revenge, or both. The assertive response would be to approach the person and honestly say that we didn't like what happened. We might then show a willingness to listen to the other person's side of the story and to discuss ways to prevent the situation's recurrence. Obviously, the latter approach will usually lead to a happier, less anxious lifestyle.

To develop appropriate assertive behavior as a way of handling problems, it is necessary to analyze the situation very carefully. We must first decide what is the proper and appropriate way of handling the situation. To do this, we must be very objective and carefully consider all the possibilities. It helps to talk it over with a

Assertion *is attacking a problem, standing up for one's rights, or doing the right thing at the right time. Aggression applies to a situation in which our attack is mixed with hostility and malice.*

To develop appropriate assertive behavior as a way of handling problems, it is necessary to analyze the situation very carefully.

friend whose judgment we trust; that person can help us think clearly. It is crucial that we let the person know that we want help in determining the appropriate way to handle the situation. Otherwise that person may try to show friendship by simply supporting us in whatever we seem to want to do, or may suggest idealistic ways of looking at the situation that sound good but won't work in practice.

Once we've decided on the appropriately assertive course of action, we need to plan in detail how we can do it and then carry out the plan. It is best to pick some easy situations in which to practice assertion and then tackle more and more difficult ones as we increase our confidence. It is also often best to start with mildly assertive behaviors and increase the strength of the assertion over time. The important thing, however, is to determine the appropriate assertive response for a given situation, plan exactly how we will do it, and then go ahead and do it. After it is over, we can analyze how it went and, if necessary, revise our plan for next time.

Let's look at an example of this. Suppose we have a job to do such as figuring our income tax for the year—a task fraught with anxiety and one that many people approach with excessive procrastination. We might analyze the situation and decide that it must be done, there is no way to get out of it. Putting it off until the last possible minute only increases the anxiety and makes it more horrendous in the end. We may then determine to take the bull by the horns, sit down, and start figuring out our income, deductions, and so on. Perhaps we'll work on it for just an hour the first night, then return to the task the next night and the next for similar periods of time until it is done. After we are in the habit of handling tasks in a mildly assertive manner such as this, we may find that we can easily be more strongly assertive in the future. For example, we may find that we can sit down and do the job in one evening instead of spreading it out in small doses over several evenings. By practicing, we can train ourselves to handle situations in an assertive rather than a procrastinating manner.

Or take another example. Suppose you have a friend who borrowed something of yours, say, a lawn mower, and failed to return it promptly. This causes you a lot of inconvenience because it is not available when you need it. A mildly assertive approach might be to tell the friend that it is fine to borrow the lawn mower and that you don't mind that, but you might go on to say that you would like it returned right after he or she has finished using it. Tell the friend that you may want to mow your own lawn, and you want it to be there in case you suddenly take a notion to cut the grass. You can of course, say this pleasantly and with a bit of humor. If you do it well, your friend will not be offended, and you will get your lawn mower back. If the friend is offended by such a simple, appropriate request, this should be looked on as the friend's problem, not yours.

A slightly stronger form of assertion might come later (if the person fails to bring the mower back after your mild attempt at assertion) or if you simply decide that you no longer want to lend your mower. The stronger form of assertion might be to tell the friend that you have decided not to lend the mower out anymore. You can explain that frequently it is not there when you need it, that it is beginning to show signs of wear, and that you don't care to put a lot of money into it for repair, and so on. You should handle the situation with tact and humor, but stand your ground. It is possible that the person may resent it, but if handled correctly, such resentment is unlikely.

One way to reduce further the possibility of the friend's being offended is to do something that shows you aren't rejecting the friendship in turning down the request; you are only setting limits in an area where you think they are needed. The way to show people they are accepted even though their requests are rejected might be to invite them in for a cup of coffee while you talk or invite them to dinner sometime later, or to compliment them for something they have done. In this manner you show them that you still value the friendship, but that you need to put some limits on the situation under discussion. A reasonable person will be able to accept and understand this.

After you have determined what action is appropriate, do it openly, honestly, and with tact and humor.

From these examples, it can be seen that assertion can be used in simple, task-oriented situations and in interpersonal situations. The technique works in more complex and emotionally charged situations as well. Deciding what is the fair and appropriate thing to do in a situation is crucial in using assertion. After you have determined what action is appropriate, do it openly, honestly, and with tact and humor.

A good thing to do after you have asserted yourself is to analyze how it went so you can learn how to handle such situations better in the future. Following this analysis, you may want to reinforce or mildly punish yourself for what you did. If you feel you did the right thing, you should say to yourself, "I did what I thought was the right thing to do in that situation. That's good. I'm glad I did that. Maybe I'm wrong, but I did what I sincerely thought was right. That's all I can do and all anyone has a right to expect of me." By doing this you reinforce your own behavior. You feel good and happy about it. If someone disagrees, you might say something like, "Well, I did what I thought was right. Tell me what you think and what you would have done." Then, without becoming anxious or upset, you will be able to discuss the other person's view and possibly get some feedback and information that will help you handle similar situations in the future. You can still rest secure in the knowledge that in the original instance you did what you thought was right, and that is all you can do—it is all anyone can do.

Sometimes a little mild self-punishment may be in order. If you handled something badly, it does no good to pretend that you didn't. It is best to say something like, "Well, I blew that one. I should have handled it differently." We should philosophically accept the fact that failure is a part of life; the important thing is to learn from our mistakes and failures so that we can do better in the future. Everybody fails once in a while. The successful person is not one who never experiences failure, but one who learns something from each failure. Viewed this way, even failures have a useful outcome.

Often after we have decided to assert ourselves in a situation, we may have trouble figuring out the best way to do it. Or we may know the best way but doubt we actually have the ability to carry it out. If we are not sure how to handle it, we can use a technique that psychologists call *modeling*. It is a basic fact that we learn a lot in life from copying other people; this is what psychologists mean by modeling. We model our behaviors by imitating what other people do, as many parents of young children have learned to their chagrin. The same principle applies in athletics. Coaches demonstrate techniques and encourage beginning athletes to watch the professionals use those techniques. Likewise, we learn much from friends, teachers, and others just by seeing what they do and trying it ourselves. This can help us learn to be properly assertive. We can observe people who assert themselves the way we would like to and see how they handle such situations ("You can see a lot just by observing," Yogi Berra once said). Later we can try the same behavior in a similar situation that involves us. We may not be too good at it the first time, but with practice we can improve. If we don't have an opportunity to observe someone in all of the situations we are interested in, we can imagine how such a person would handle it.

Modeling can help us learn to be properly assertive.

Earlier in this book, we talked about behavior rehearsal, which is practicing behavior before we try it in a given situation. That approach works very well with assertion. We can practice alone, possibly in front of a mirror. Or we can get someone to play the other part and help us. Practice makes us more skilled and better able to behave naturally when the situation calls for it.

Another aid to assertive behavior is reading some of the books on positive thinking. Such books as *The Power of Positive Thinking,* by Norman Vincent Peale; *How to Win Friends and Influence People,* by Dale Carnegie; and *Psycho-Cybernetics,* by Maxwell Maltz, can be very helpful. There are a number of such books in the library and available as paperbacks in the bookstores. If these books have a flaw it is that they lead us to believe that if only we have a positive attitude, everything will turn out all right. This is a little too simple. It often takes more than positive thinking; it may also take the right circumstances, the right behavior, ability, help from others, and so on. All other things being equal, however, situations end on a better note when we think positively. Such thinking helps us make the best of most situations and facilitates success, even if it is not in itself enough to assure that success. Books on positive thinking often contain helpful hints on ways to assert yourself and provide support and encouragement to go ahead and try. They are well worth reading if we keep them in perspective. There are also good books on developing assertion skills, such as *Your Perfect Right,* by Robert Alberti and Michael Emmons; *Responsible Assertive Behavior,* by A. Lange and P. Jakubowski; *Don't Say Yes When You Want to Say No,* by Herbert Fensterheim and Jean Baer; or *The New Assertive Woman,* by Lynn Z. Bloom, Karen Coburn, and Joan Pearlman.

STRESS MANAGEMENT EXERCISES

1. Pick a small task that does not involve interpersonal relationships (e.g., cleaning your desk, attic, garage, or something similar) over which you tend to procrastinate. Develop a plan to practice assertion with respect to this task. Break the task into segments, if necessary; decide how to do it; obtain any needed materials in advance; schedule a time to get started on it; and just *do* it. Write down your thoughts after carrying out your plan. Did you feel better and more relaxed afterward?

_____

_____

_____

_____

_____

_____

_____

_____

_____

_____

_____

_____

_____

2. Pick a small task that does involve interpersonal relationships and develop a plan to be assertive about it. For example, it might be handling someone who frequently is inconsiderate when a decision is being made; saying no to a salesperson; or setting limits with a person. Decide how to handle the situation with tact and humor. Practice it in front of a mirror and then do it. To the inconsiderate person, you might say, "Wait. You always pick the restaurant that we go to. There are several that I have been wanting to try. Let me list some I am interested in and you pick one." For the salesperson, you might go into a store where you do not need to make a purchase. When the salesperson approaches, say, "I am just looking, thanks." If he or she says anything more, repeat your statement, nothing more. To set a limit, try, "I'm having trouble managing things, so I am making a rule for myself that I won't answer the phone after 10:00 P.M. Either call me before then or leave a message." Write how your effort worked. How can you do better next time?

_____

_____

_____

_____

_____

_____

_____

_____

_____

_____

_____

_____

3. Pick a more complicated interpersonal situation in which you need to be assertive. Talk it over with a friend to be sure you are being fair to the other person. With the help of the friend, develop a strategy for being assertive and then use behavior rehearsal to prepare for the real event. In the rehearsal, you be the person that you need to talk to and have your friend play your part. Then switch roles. Discuss what seemed to work and what didn't. Approach the person using the strategy and techniques you developed. Don't forget to use tact and humor. Also, take a few deep breaths to relax before you approach the person. Usually one's first efforts at assertion are only partial successes; it gets better with practice. Write a description of how this effort went and how to do better next time.

_____

_____

_____

_____

_____

_____

_____

_____

_____

_____

_____

_____

_____

_____

_____

_____

_____

_____

_____

_____

_____

_____

_____

_____

_____

_____

_____

_____

4. Pick a person who is very skilled at asserting himself or herself in a situation in which you think you need to improve. Watch what that person does and use him or her as a model. Practice in front of a mirror doing what the model does, then do it yourself in real life. It's common to feel awkward and phony the first couple of times doing something the way another person does it; however, soon it will feel natural and will be a part of you. Describe your attempt and analyze it to see how it can be improved.

_____

_____

_____

_____

_____

_____

_____

_____

_____

_____

_____

_____

_____

5. In the following space, write a few notes about the difference between assertion and aggression. Which works best? How do you feel after using one or the other? Do you notice a reduction in anxiety when you use assertion properly?

_____

_____

_____

_____

_____

_____

_____

_____

_____

_____

_____

_____

_____

9

Problem Solving, Decision Making, and Brainstorming

OFTEN ACUTE ANXIETY develops when we are faced with solving problems or making decisions. This can be true of any type of decision, but it is especially true of important ones. We find ourselves struggling with the problem of deciding. One minute we feel one way, the next minute we feel another way. We worry that maybe we'll make the wrong decision, and we wish there were some way to determine the right thing to do. The more we put off making the decision, the more anxious we get. We know that we must decide, but we don't know what to do. The tension becomes excruciating. We can't sleep. We lose our appetite and become preoccupied with the decision we have to make. Some people have this kind of difficulty with both little and big decisions. Other people have problems making decisions in some matters but not in others. In this chapter, we will examine some ways to make good decisions, and to make them less painfully.

One simple way is to sit down and try to make the process more concrete. Often we have a number of vague ideas, fears, concerns, and so on, in our heads, but because we have not really put them into words, they are hard to handle. A good procedure is to sit down with a piece of paper and draw a line down the middle. Put

We find ourselves struggling with the problem of deciding.

the reasons for a certain course of action (pros) on one side and the reasons against the action (cons) on the other. Study the two lists and try to weigh your feelings. Often putting the reasons into words clarifies our thinking, and seeing the words on paper helps us weigh the alternatives and decide. Sometimes it helps to make the list of pros and cons and put it away for a while. When you come back later, the decision may seem to have made itself. Or you may add or subtract from the list and then make the decision. At any rate, this technique does help clarify your thinking and moves you toward actually making the decision instead of just thinking about it in a vague, disorganized manner.

A technique for problem solving and decision making that was pioneered by Alex Osborn is called *brainstorming*. The process of brainstorming is quite simple and effective. Basically a procedure for groups, it can also be used as an individual technique. To use it in groups, get some people together who are interested and co-operative (about 5–10 seems to work best, but often 2 or 3 will work). Specify as clearly as possible exactly on what problem the session is to focus. Then start generating ideas according to the four basic rules for brainstorming.

1. *No judgment of ideas.* Criticism of your own ideas or of the ideas of other people is stifling and inhibits creativity. It is not permitted during the brainstorming session, but will come later.

2. *Free-wheeling is encouraged.* Try to come up with wild, unusual ideas. Ideas that are new and different are wanted. After all, if conventional or obvious ideas contained easy solutions, you would not have been so stumped by the problem. It is often possible to take a wild idea and tame it, making it a very creative and valuable solution to a problem.

3. *Quantity, not quality.* Your goal as a group is to come up with as many ideas as possible. Research has shown that more good ideas can be developed by expressing *all* the ideas that come to us, rather than expressing only the "good" ones.

4. *Combine and improve.* As each person's ideas are expressed, group members should think of ways to extend, revise, or combine them with other ideas to produce still *other* ideas or combinations. In generating and revising ideas, consider such points as: To what other uses could we put this object or idea in its present form (uses that have not been thought of or tried before)? What uses would be possible if we somehow adapted or modified the object or idea? What would happen if we maximized or minimized one aspect or effect? What if we changed the order and did it in a different sequence?

There is good evidence that using brainstorming techniques produces excellent results. It seems that one person's thoughts and ideas often stir another's associations, stimulating that person to come up with ideas and thoughts that would not have occurred in isolation, and vice versa. Further, the social motivation of working on a problem with a group of people enables us to work more diligently and enthusiastically than we would on our own. Finally, competition and friendly rivalry seem to stimulate greater productivity.

There is an old story about the community stew. One neighbor had carrots; another had a potato; another, a piece of meat; and so on. If everyone had stayed home, they all would have had a meager, unbalanced diet—but when they got together in the town square and put what they had in one pot, there was enough for a feast for everyone.

If you want to use group brainstorming to work on a problem, get a number of people together who are as motivated and concerned about the problem as you are. They might be friends who have interests similar to yours. If the problem is job related, they might be people you work with or are at least in a similar line of work. They might be family members if it is a family problem. (Incidentally, don't hesitate to include children in such sessions. Often they come up with some outstandingly fresh and creative

If you want to use group brainstorming to work on a problem, get a number of people together who are as motivated and concerned about the problem as you are.

approaches.) It is interesting to brainstorm such things as income-tax deductions, ways to save money around the house, or how to get a job done more quickly and easily.

While two heads are better than one, and groups are better brainstormers than individuals are, it is not impossible to do it alone. You can. Just sit quietly and let ideas flow, following the four rules mentioned earlier. You can do it at home or in your office; while traveling somewhere or any other time. The main value of brainstorming is that it generates ideas—and one thing that hinders decision making is the inhibition of ideas. This is often because the person has become too rigid. To be rigid in your thinking means that you can see only one or two ways of approaching a problem and are not able to look at it from different points of view. If one of the limited solutions you contrive works, then everything is fine; if not, you are in trouble. Such rigid thinking often leads to anxiety over problems that can be solved easily if we can break out of the rigid mold in which we find ourselves. As ideas are generated during brainstorming, it is best simply to jot them down as they come. Do not go over them or evaluate them until later—then prepare a new list containing some of the better ones. After some study and thought, prepare a new list by putting what you consider the best alternative at the top and the least desirable one at the bottom. That way, you can try the first one and see if it works. If it does, you have solved the problem; if it does not, go to the next alternative and continue in this manner until you find one that works.

Ordering the alternatives by desirability requires you to consider several features of each alternative, which is, of course, the hardest part of the task. You may have heard the old story about the farmhand who worked diligently for his boss. When he was in the fields, nobody could keep up with him; he could do twice as much as the other farmhands, and he seemed to enjoy and thrive on hard work. One day when it was particularly hot the boss decided to give the farmhand a break. He called him from the fields and took him into the barn where it was cool and where he could sit down. His job for the day was to sort the potatoes according to size into three piles—small, medium, and large. At the end of the day, the boss came back and was shocked to see that his best worker was sitting dejectedly in the corner. He had hardly sorted any potatoes at all! Puzzled, he asked him what the problem was. The man replied, "It's these damned decisions."

One of the first things to consider in ordering the possible alternatives is their degree of reversibility. There are some that you can try, and if they don't work, no particular harm will have been done. You can simply go on to another one. But some of the alternatives, once tried, make further solutions harder or impossible to accomplish. Such alternatives generally should be placed farther down on the list.

A second consideration is the amount of effort required to try a solution. If it is easy to do, it may be worth trying and should be placed closer to the top of the list than one that is difficult or that takes a lot of time and effort.

A third consideration is the risk involved. If an alternative is attempted, what are the risks? What are things that might go wrong, and what would be the consequences if they did? Obviously, risky alternatives will tend to fit lower on the list.

A fourth consideration is the probability that the solution will work. Some are long shots, and others are almost sure things. This needs to be taken into account.

Finally, keeping the previous considerations in mind, we must consider the ultimate payoff. If we try a given solution and it works, how will it benefit us?

These principles, you will find, tend to be combined in different ways in each of the possible alternatives. With some thought, we can order them according to preference and begin to try them. I often like to start with a long shot that doesn't take too much effort, is completely reversible, and that would have a large payoff—if such an alternative exists. If you don't have a dream, it can't come true. If you try for your dream, you may achieve it; if not, however, proceed down the list. The solutions I put on the bottom are ones that require a lot of effort, are irreversible, and, though pretty certain to work, tend to have minimal payoff.

Different people may choose different strategies, and any one person may use different strategies in different situations. The important thing is to have a strategy and to execute it. Some people find it helpful to write the list of alternatives and check them off as they are tried; others just keep the alternatives in mind. Putting them down on paper often makes one feel better and facilitates clear thought and action.

The important thing is to have a strategy and to execute it.

There are some additional principles of decision making that are well to keep in mind. One is that in the majority of the situations we face, only we can really make the decision. Relying on somebody else to tell us what to do will generally not lead to satisfactory results. As is often said, advice is easy to give but hard to take. If a whole group happens to be involved, we may want to make the decision by committee vote, but the majority of decisions that we face and that produce anxiety are matters only we can decide. We may as well face up to this and do so assertively.

Second, we need to realize that we sometimes will make what seems like the wrong decision. Actually, if we follow the principles outlined in this chapter, it will not be wrong; we will have made the best decision possible under the circumstances. Sometimes, however, the outcome may not be what we wanted. When that happens, we need to accept the fact that everybody wins some and loses some—ourselves included. The main point is to learn from each experience so that we ultimately win more than we lose.

Third, it helps a great deal if we practice reinforcing ourselves after we have made a decision. To do this, we can say something to ourselves like, "Well, I made the best decision possible as the situation presented itself. That's all I could do. I did what I thought was right and that's what a person ought to do. I'm glad I did it. I fulfilled my responsibility." Later, if someone else has a different idea or if things don't turn out the way you wanted, you can be open to learning from the situation. You need not feel defensive or upset because you have already settled the matter within yourself. You honestly and sincerely did what you considered to be the right thing and you can feel good about that part. If a revision is called for, you are free to go ahead with that as part two of the process; you will then reinforce yourself for that part as well.

The point is that you are monitoring your own behavior and doing what you think is right. This makes you a person of integrity and self-confidence. You are receptive to feedback from others, but you make up your own mind. It is this balance that makes a mature, responsible person. If we are overly stubborn about our ideas, we are not fair to others. If we are overly dependent on what others think we ought to do in a situation, we are wishy-washy and lack personal integrity. This makes us anxious and miserable. Successful decision making takes a balance of responsiveness to feedback and internal judgment. The fulcrum is self-reinforcement.

Successful decision making takes a balance of responsiveness to feedback and internal judgment.

STRESS MANAGEMENT EXERCISES

1. Pick a problem about which you must make a decision. Using the technique described on pages 141–142, make a worksheet to deal with this decision. Write the pros to the left and the cons to the right.

Pros	Cons

2. Now write your decision in the following space. Wait a week and look at the decision again. If it still seems like a good idea, put it into action.

_____

_____

_____

_____

_____

_____

_____

_____

_____

_____

_____

_____

_____

3. Jot down some thoughts or insights you learned from Exercise 2.

_____

_____

_____

_____

_____

_____

_____

_____

_____

_____

_____

4. Pick a problem to brainstorm by yourself. Write all of your ideas about the problem in the following space—but *do not* evaluate or analyze them!

_____

_____

_____

_____

_____

_____

_____

_____

_____

_____

_____

_____

_____

_____

_____

_____

_____

_____

_____

_____

_____

_____

_____

_____

5. Now go back and analyze the options. Edit and revise them into a list of possible alternatives as described on page 145.

_____

_____

_____

_____

_____

_____

_____

_____

_____

_____

_____

_____

_____

_____

_____

_____

_____

_____

_____

_____

_____

_____

_____

_____

_____

6. Choose your first alternative and try it out, then write down the result. Did it work? If so, congratulate yourself and celebrate. If not, try to figure out why. Then, try it again or go to the next alternative and the next until one of them works. Keep track of your attempts in the following space.

_____

_____

_____

_____

_____

_____

_____

_____

_____

_____

_____

_____

_____

_____

_____

_____

_____

_____

_____

_____

_____

_____

_____

_____

_____

_____

_____

7. Jot down your thoughts or insights gained from your brainstorming.

_____

_____

_____

_____

_____

_____

_____

_____

_____

_____

_____

_____

_____

8. Consider using brainstorming in a small group for a common problem, and write about the experience.

_____

_____

_____

_____

_____

_____

_____

_____

_____

_____

_____

_____

_____

_____

_____

_____

_____

_____

_____

_____

_____

_____

9. Ask some of the members of the group to share their thoughts about the brain-storming and record their remarks as well.

_____

_____

_____

_____

_____

_____

_____

_____

_____

_____

_____

_____

_____

_____

10. As you begin to employ these techniques, do you notice a reduction in anxiety about decision making and a growth in your self-confidence? Write your thoughts about this.

_____

_____

_____

_____

_____

_____

_____

_____

_____

_____

_____

_____

_____

_____

1 0

Nutrition and Exercise

WHEN I WAS A BOY going to school in Madison, Ohio, we used to have a grade-school teacher named Pop Ryan. He was about 70 years old but was in excellent health and full of vigor. He was a man of the old school and used to lecture us on the importance of maintaining good health and hygiene practices—the old "sound mind in a healthy body" theory. We used to snicker at him while eating excessive quantities of hamburgers and french fries, with a soft drink to wash them down. We knew our diets would have caused his hair to stand on end, but we regarded him as sort of a kook. It's funny, though, over the years, as I learned more and more about physical and mental health, I began to discover that Pop Ryan had something. I've found in terms of my own experience and in clinical work with my patients that physical and mental health often go together.

When we are tense, anxious, and depressed, we feel physical pain and general malaise. Also when we are physically ill—for example when we come down with a cold or the flu—we often feel emotionally upset, depressed, and anxious. Good physical health contributes to good mental health and vice versa.

Consider general nutrition. Food has special significance for

Physical and mental health often go together.

many people. Since we are often comforted with food as children, we tend to associate food with love and security. Thus, many people find that they eat when they are anxious or tense. Eating makes them feel better temporarily. It is interesting to note that certain kinds of food prepared in certain ways may have the same effect. For example, many people find that very spicy foods, such as Italian or Mexican dishes, tend to cause discomfort. This may be the effect of such foods on some people, but I was reared on food prepared by a wonderful Italian mother. As a result, eating spicy foods actually has a calming and settling effect on my stomach. Some of my physiologically oriented friends tell me that isn't possible, yet it works that way for me.

Various claims are made from time to time that certain foods such as organically grown foods or uncooked food, or some special diet such as a strictly vegetarian diet, will result in better physical health and possibly improve mental health. Because many of these claims have not been thoroughly studied, there is no scientific evidence to support them at present. But research is going on in many areas related to nutrition and health, and this research is shedding new light on nutrition's relationship to the brain's activities.

One notion currently being explored is that a person may suffer from cerebral allergies; just as one can develop a runny nose or a skin rash after contact with a substance to which he or she is allergic, the brain can react to chemicals circulating in the bloodstream in a similar manner. We know that the brain is richly supplied with blood vessels; thus, any substance in the bloodstream can potentially influence brain function. It is speculated that eating certain foods to which one has a cerebral allergy might result in agitation, anxiety, depression, or some other mental symptom. Unfortunately there is no scientific evidence to support this theory in the form stated. What makes these theories plausible is that some very general relationships between ingesting certain foods and the function of the brain have been known for some time. For example, excessive consumption of beverages with caffeine can produce nervousness, anxiety, and irritability. Likewise, some recent research indicates that consumption of foods containing carbohydrates can have a calming and sedating effect on an individual.

While some very general relationships of this sort have been carefully documented, the vast majority have not survived rigorous scientific research. For example, there has been considerable research on the relationship between sugar and activity levels in children. The overwhelming evidence in this area is that, contrary to many claims made, sugar consumption does not produce hyperactivity in children, nor do food colorings, products containing wheat, or other substances. We may discover that there are subgroups of individuals who respond to certain foods differently than other people do; however, most researchers in the area of nutrition do not expect dramatic findings of this sort.

At present, trained nutritionists are cautious about making any claims for such eating habits until there is sound scientific support for them. What is important to remember meanwhile is that nutritional deficiencies result in declining health and even disease, which are often accompanied by mental and emotional symptoms of one sort or another. Therefore, a well-balanced diet contributes to the general energy level, stamina, and sense of well being in an individual.

Nutritional deficiencies result in declining health and even disease, which are often accompanied by mental and emotional symptoms of one sort or another.

Many of the rules for good nutrition that are generally endorsed by physicians and nutritionists are aimed at avoiding obesity. Since you were a child you've been taught to eat a balanced diet each day. A balanced diet is one that includes the four basic food groups of (a) milk, cheese, and other dairy products, (b) meat, (c) vegetables and fruit, and (d) bread and cereals. Almost any diet book on the market will caution you to reduce intake of animal fat; avoid too many fried foods and sweets; to eat more, smaller meals rather than fewer, larger ones; and to eat slowly, chewing food carefully.

You should also make mealtime a time for relaxing. Rather than eating hurriedly, gulping your food and conducting business during meals, try taking a walk, reading, resting, listening to music, or some such activity to unwind a little before it's time to eat.

Make mealtime a time for relaxing.

Then sit down and enjoy a leisurely, relaxed meal. You'll enjoy the food much more, take the edge off daily anxiety, and reduce the likelihood of developing gastric problems.

There is currently some debate about nutrition in the United States. Some say our food storage and preparation methods reduce the nutritional value of the food we consume. Others insist that we are the healthiest and best-fed people who have ever lived. Still others say that while perfectly adequate foods are available to Americans, their eating habits do not provide them with the proper selection to produce a balanced diet. Nutritionists say that following a balanced diet (which includes foods from each of the basic groups) is sufficient for most people's good health, and that no further supplements such as health foods or vitamins are needed. However, one might wish to take one multivitamin/mineral tablet per day of the type designed for such use. Anything beyond that should be done with consultation from your physician or a trained nutritionist.

There is a lot of faddism in this area. Physicians are quick to point out that fad diets, large doses of vitamins, and similar practices may be dangerous and harmful to some people. Therefore, if you feel you need a dietary supplement, consult a physician who is trained in nutrition; your family physician can help you locate one. The doctor can examine you and prescribe the right supplement or medication if you need it. Doing this will enable you to get exactly what you need in a safe, supervised manner. Experimenting on your own can be dangerous.

Exercise is also very effective in reducing anxiety, although how this occurs is not entirely understood. Some say that it satisfies our innate need to engage our large muscles in physically aggressive activity. In primitive times we had natural outlets for this kind of activity, but in our highly civilized, sedentary, and confined lifestyle we do not. More recently, researchers have begun to discover changes in body chemistry following exercise that may explain our changes in mood. Physiologically, exercise affects all the systems of the body. Circulation of blood and consumption of oxygen are increased. Body temperature rises. Metabolism is stepped up. Waste products are excreted more rapidly from the cells and are eventually eliminated from the body through perspiration, urination, and defecation.

Prolonged and intensive exercise tends to increase the level of lactic acid in the blood. Although such an increase is usually associated with anxiety, when secreted during exercise, lactic acid seems to reduce anxiety and tension. This may be related to the fact that the body produces chemicals called *endorphins* under such circumstances. Endorphins act on the body much as morphine does, reducing pain and promoting a feeling of well-being. Endorphins probably account for what has been called *runner's high,* in which individuals who run or exercise vigorously for prolonged periods of time may experience a state of euphoria that occurs long after the start of exercise, when one might expect the individual to be feeling extreme fatigue and pain. The natural endorphins produced by the body, no doubt, are producing a high that might be induced under other circumstances by drugs. A very similar state is often achieved by individuals who engage in meditation and yoga. To date, there haven't been extensive scientific studies of endorphin levels in individuals who have reached states of euphoria by these means. It is clear, however, that endorphins play a major part in many of the experiences of well-being that are associated with exercise.

Endorphins play a major part in many of the experiences of well-being that are associated with exercise.

Many people find it worthwhile to meditate during strenuous exercise, such as running, or immediately afterward. Again, the release of endorphins may well facilitate the process of meditation. Books by Kenneth Cooper, MD, such as *New Aerobics* or the *Aerobics Program for Total Well-Being,* both of which are available in paperback, can be helpful in planning a program of the type discussed in this chapter.

Over a period of time, exercise increases vital capacity. Circulation and oxygen utilization are improved, and a larger exertion is required before lactic acid is produced. It is possible that in this way exercise serves as a sort of anxiety-inhibiting mechanism. Whatever its basis, exercise does have an anxiety- and tension-reducing effect. Studies have shown that people on regular exercise programs tend to be more healthy, have better vital capacity, handle problems better, sleep better, and cope with life in a generally more satisfactory manner. Over a period of time, people on such programs tend to feel better, to be more optimistic, and to have a better self-image. Thus exercise reduces anxiety somewhat right away, and over the long run, it tends to inoculate us against development of future anxieties.

Exercise, however, can be very dangerous if too strenuous or of the wrong type for a person's physical condition. In general, the older you are the more cautious you need to be, but youth is not guaranteed protection against injury. Every year young people engaged in athletic activities suffer heart attacks, strokes, and other complications. Before beginning an exercise program, it is important to consult your family physician for advice.

There are two basic types of exercise that can be employed to reduce anxiety: rhythmic motion and stretching

There are two basic types of exercise that can be employed to reduce anxiety. One is rhythmic motion. Walking, running, swimming, and bicycling provide rhythmic motion; jogging has become a popular exercise of this type. Cooper's aerobics programs are very good. As he points out, such exercise not only reduces anxiety, it also increases general health, aids in weight reduction, and helps prevent heart disease and various other disorders.

The other major type of exercise that can reduce anxiety is stretching. You may have noticed that people frequently stretch their arms above their heads in times of tension to help relieve discomfort. You can elaborate on this basic technique. For example, if you feel tension in the neck, take your head in your hands and gently stretch your neck. Then hold the head and chin and exert pressure downward, again stretching the neck muscles. If the back is tense, bend and stretch in ways that gently pull the muscles. If your chest muscles are tight, make some stretching movements with the arms in various directions until the tension and tightness subside. Practicing exercises of this sort on a regular basis can be very beneficial. You can even ask your physician to refer you to a physical therapist for specific instructions on stretching exercises.

When I encourage patients to exercise for anxiety reduction, I generally point out to them that to do the most good the exercise should be a regular activity. Therefore, it should be worked into their daily routines. Many people exercise first thing in the morning, then take a shower and go to work. A friend of mine who was a university professor used to jog from his home to the university. He had a locker in the gym where he showered and dressed for classes after he arrived. Some people exercise when they get home from work or just before bedtime (for some people exercise before bed causes sleep problems, but for others it seems to facilitate sleep). Most cities of any size have groups who get together during their lunch hour at the YMCA or at one of the commercial health centers, and some companies provide exercise facilities for their employees.

Whenever or wherever one does it, *regular* exercise is the key. If you have other physical problems, your physician or a physical therapist can recommend specific exercises to work into your routine. For example, I have a shoulder that pops out of place easily and an old back injury from high school. Both tend to give me a lot of pain from time to time. I consulted a physical therapist and learned some exercises to incorporate into my usual program. When I do these exercises regularly, my shoulder stays in place and my back gives me no trouble. As fellow sufferers know, these are no small benefits.

Because many people can't get excited about rising an hour earlier to jog or about giving up their lunch hour to do so, I recommend that they choose a sport they like and play it regularly for exercise. Tennis, handball, golf, and swimming are just a few sports that can help you relax. Be sure to consult a physician before you begin an exercise program. Then start out gradually and build up your endurance rather than trying to do too much too soon. The goal should be to develop a program involving a minimum of 20 to 30 minutes at least every other day. More is better, when you are physically ready for it.

Many people find hot baths to be very relaxing. The heat increases circulation, accelerates the metabolic activity of cells, carries away waste products more rapidly, and relaxes muscle tissue. It is a purgative process. While the reason is not fully understood, pain is also reduced under these circumstances. Whirlpool baths are even more effective. Small whirlpool units can be purchased for home use and most exercise centers have them. The whirlpool turbines circulate the water, adding gentle massage to the benefits of the heat. Some people find alternating hot and cold water to be very relaxing. First take a hot bath or shower and stay under the hot water for 4 or 5 minutes. Then turn the hot water off and turn cold water on for about 2 minutes. This can be harmful to some people, however, especially if they have any type of circulatory problem, and it is best to check with your physician before you try this.

Sauna and steam baths are other ways to enjoy the benefits of heat. If you plan to use sauna or steam baths, it is important to familiarize yourself with the equipment and use it properly. Talk to someone familiar with the equipment you are using and read the manufacturer's manual. In general, the rules for safe use of sauna and steam baths are as follows. First, remember that sauna and steam baths can be dangerous for some people—the elderly and people suffering from diabetes, heart disease, high blood pressure, and other conditions. In addition, you could be in danger if you ingest alcohol, antihistamines, anticoagulants, narcotics, tranquilizers, sedatives, or other medications before a sauna or steam bath. Therefore, as with other activities suggested in this chapter, you should consult your physician before you begin. A phone call to your family physician will suffice; if you do not have one, use this as a good opportunity to get a physical exam and discuss your plans with the physician who examines you.

Second, be sure to read and follow the directions of the equipment manufacturer or of the person supervising the equipment. Do not use the equipment alone. Someone should be around to help if necessary. There should be a window for the person to check on you, and there should be a clock clearly visible so you will know how long you have been in. If you are a beginner, start out with just a couple of minutes, no more than 5. Gradually increase to a level that feels good. Never stay in more than 20 to 30 minutes. Do not exercise strenuously before sauna or steam baths, and do not exercise at all while in them. Stay out of them for at least an hour after eating a full meal, and drink liquids before and after.

Proper use of sauna and steam baths will reduce weight (though it is only water loss and will return shortly), increase circulation, lead to muscular relaxation, and possibly improve and clear the skin. There is no evidence that they prevent or cure the common cold. They are not recommended for people whose sinuses are draining or as a cure for a hangover.

Massage can have a similarly relaxing and beneficial effect. Massage increases circulation and metabolism in the same way heat does, and it appears to offer additional advantages. The mechanics of massage force fluid out of the tissues, thus reducing swelling and pressure due to the excessive fluid that sometimes gathers after trauma or exercise. Also, the mechanical stretching of the muscles and connective tissues tends to relax them and reduce pain. Massage must be done properly to be of much help. Most health centers and many YMCAs and similar clubs have trained masseurs available; physical therapists also provide massage. Generally, a referral from a physician is required before a physical therapist can see you, but this is not hard to obtain. In smaller towns, a nurse, a physical-education teacher, or a trainer for school athletes can provide massage. Many people find that a good massage reduces anxiety remarkably and makes them feel like a new person.

My experience has been that it takes a lot of encouragement to get people to try the things mentioned in this chapter, but that when they do, they invariably report that the techniques work and that they had never felt better in their lives. These techniques appear to reduce anxiety as well as improve general health and stamina. A regular program can involve minutes or hours per day, but it appears to be time well spent.

A regular program can involve minutes or hours per day, but it appears to be time well spent.

STRESS MANAGEMENT EXERCISES

1. Keep a food diary for one month. Write down everything you eat (including all snacks, etc.). Are you surprised about what you are eating? Evaluate your diet by using some reputable reference works (e.g., *American Heart Association Cookbook,* Ballantine Books) or by discussing it with your physician or a trained nutritional therapist. Write your evaluation here.

_____

_____

_____

_____

_____

_____

_____

_____

_____

_____

_____

_____

_____

_____

_____

_____

_____

_____

_____

_____

_____

_____

_____

_____

_____

2. Develop a plan for better eating habits and write it in the following space.

_____

_____

_____

_____

_____

_____

_____

_____

_____

_____

_____

_____

_____

_____

_____

_____

_____

_____

_____

_____

_____

_____

_____

_____

_____

_____

_____

_____

3. Consider the circumstances under which you eat each meal of the day. If any of them are eaten in haste or under pressure, develop a plan to make them more relaxing. In particular, pick one meal to be a family or friend time. Structure that meal so that it is a time of fellowship and communication around food, and write down your experiences with this.

_____

_____

_____

_____

_____

_____

_____

_____

_____

_____

_____

_____

_____

_____

4. Do you have cravings for food, or eat compulsively? If so, write about these here. Consider discussing them with a mental health professional or a nutritional therapist.

_____

_____

_____

_____

_____

_____

_____

_____

_____

_____

_____

_____

_____

_____

_____

_____

_____

5. How do emotions affect your eating? When you are depressed or anxious are you likely to eat more or to lose your appetite? Is this something to discuss with a mental health professional? Write about your thoughts on this.

_____

_____

_____

_____

_____

_____

_____

_____

_____

_____

_____

_____

_____

6. Describe in writing your exercise habits. The general recommendation is that one should engage in 20 to 30 minutes of vigorous, but not overly strenuous, exercise per day. How would you evaluate your habits?

_____

_____

_____

_____

_____

_____

_____

_____

_____

_____

_____

7. Develop a plan for playing a sport, jogging, brisk walking, swimming, or some other form of exercise that you can do for 20 or 30 minutes per day. You may need to begin with fewer minutes and build from there. If you have any health problems or limitations, you should consult your physician about the type and amount of exercise that is best for you. Write out your plan here.

_____

_____

_____

_____

_____

_____

_____

_____

_____

_____

_____

_____

_____

_____

_____

_____

_____

_____

8. Start to follow the plan developed in Exercise 7. Remember, it often helps to exercise with a friend—the social motivation helps you stick with it. Keep track of your mood as you exercise. Use a scale of 0 (worst mood you have ever been in) to 100 (best you have ever felt) and record your general mood for the day in the following space. Do this daily for a month. Did you experience a general elevation in mood over the time you have been keeping track?

_____

_____

_____

_____

_____

_____

_____

_____

_____

_____

_____

_____

_____

_____

_____

_____

_____

9. Find a place where you can try each of the following: steam bath, sauna, hot tub. Which did you enjoy the most? Do you think you might like to do this more often?

_____

_____

_____

_____

_____

_____

_____

_____

_____

_____

_____

_____

10. Treat yourself to a professional massage (be careful that it is a legitimate service and not a front for illegal sexual activity). Write about your physical and emotional feelings following the experience. Is this something you would like to do periodically?

_____

_____

_____

_____

I I

Recreation and Escape

ANXIOUS PEOPLE DON'T have much fun in life. When we are anxious, we suffer such mental anguish and physical pain that we cannot enjoy ourselves. It is also true that if we do not make provisions for having fun, we become more susceptible to anxiety. These two facts tend to reinforce each other, and eventually we get into a terrible rut. We are anxious so much of the time that we can't enjoy ourselves, and not enjoying ourselves tends to make us more anxious and depressed.

A number of factors can trigger this cycle. Often it starts with very real tensions and problems that, if left unresolved, eventually get us down; then we get into the anxiety rut. Paradoxically, we sometimes become so familiar with our anxiety rut that we are afraid to venture out of it. Other alternatives seem vague, unfamiliar, and even more threatening. (The devil you know is less frightening than the one you don't.) Sam Keen puts it almost poetically. In his book *To a Dancing God* (New York: Harper & Row, 1970, pp. 109–110), he records a dialogue he had with fear. Part of it goes like this:

Sam Keen: I wish I could begin by saying, "Damn you fear. Leave me alone!" But honesty demands that I address you as

When we are anxious, we suffer such mental anguish and physical pain that we cannot enjoy ourselves.

"Dear fear," for you have been with me most of my life. Now I want to understand why I am attracted to you and did not banish you long ago.

Fear: I am glad you are willing to admit that we are reluctant friends. It has taken me some years to get you to confess that you are a hesitant lover of what you pretend to despise. What a capacity for self-deceit you have, pretending that I was somehow your fated enemy! Or, to be specific, that I was an unconscious legacy from your parents. Such transparent nonsense. If I am your fate, I am at least a fate you have chosen and nurtured. It is not without your consent and satisfaction that we have been together all these years. You might have lived in conversation with love, or courage, or creativity, or desire, or fame. No! You have kept me around. So don't try to disown me.

Sometimes we get into an anxiety rut by failing simply to play. Our society teaches that work is good and play, for adults, is evil. It is a sinful waste of time and talent. As we become adults, we are supposed to grow out of our need for play; if we don't, we are stupid and immature. The ultimate believer in this has been called a *workaholic*. A workaholic is a person who is not happy if he or she is not working at something. Such a person can't get enough of it to be satisfied, and may work long hours at one, two, or more jobs. When this person goes home, work from the office is taken along and he or she thinks of things to do around the house. Idle time makes a workaholic nervous. Weekends are an agony and vacations drag because he or she can't wait to get back to work. Even people who do not work outside the house often show the same pattern, working at home from early morning until late at night, seven days a week. Such a person may attend to house and family excessively. No time is left for resting.

Workaholics have many of the same problems as alcoholics. Their obsession with work destroys their families and interpersonal lives, ruins their health, and eventually leaves them desolate. In many cases, such people would actually have been more productive in the long run if they had not overworked themselves early in life.

As has often been pointed out, the word *recreation* means literally re-creation. The respite and escape we derive from play refreshes us and makes us able to go back and work more later. It enables us to be more productive longer. It is interesting that a very common symptom of emotional disturbance is withdrawal. People who are emotionally disturbed often isolate themselves from friends, renege on responsibilities, and turn off life. Such people become unresponsive, uncommunicative, and unproductive. What has happened at this point is that problems have overwhelmed them and they are unable to handle them. Thus, they retreat from the problems and give up completely. As with many of the symptoms of emotional disturbance, this massive retreat from life is just an exaggeration of a more normal response common to everyone. We all need to get away from our problems and responsibilities from time to time. Play and recreation can be a tactical retreat, enabling us to come back better and stronger later. If we use recreation that way, massive retreat into emotional disturbance will not be necessary. As Oscar Wilde whimsically put it, "Life is far too important to be taken seriously."

Thus, to live a productive life and keep anxiety at a minimum, you need adequate recreation and escape. There are many ways to find these things. First, you need to relearn the way to play. If you have been anxious for a long time or are a veteran workaholic, you may have to reach back into the past and search your memory to find things you can do for play (if you really think about it, you *can* come up with some). It is important that you begin to do things *you* like to do and that give *you* pleasure. They may be things you've always wanted to do but for which you couldn't seem to find time. Some people enjoy walks or hikes. Others like to play a sport such as tennis or golf. Some like to go on picnics, whereas others would rather try out a new restaurant. Some people go to plays or

"Life is far too important to be taken seriously."
—OSCAR WILDE

movies for escape. Others prefer athletic events. Some take one-
or two-day trips out of town; others prefer to stay home and play
a family game or watch TV. Many people like to shop or browse.
Some like to cook. Others like to listen to music or play an instrument. There are hundreds of things people do for recreation.
You should do some of the ones you like.

If it has been so long since you did them that you really don't
feel like it, force yourself. You have to start somewhere. When you
engage in these activities, practice clearing your mind of all that
has been preoccupying you. Then become totally absorbed in the
activity you have chosen. It takes a little effort and practice to be
able to do that, but you can train yourself to do so. *Thought stopping,* mentioned in Chapter 5, is often helpful in keeping the mind
clear of thoughts that would prevent us from enjoying play. Once
you learn to put worries out of your mind and become absorbed
in play, you will find that these activities provide great satisfaction
and enjoyment. They will add a new dimension of richness to your
life. You will begin to see them as islands of refuge and refreshment. If you do them frequently, they become a major source of
pleasure. You will continually think of the fun of the last experience and look forward to the next. This makes life more exciting
and enables us to do a better job at the more difficult tasks we face.

Developing a hobby can serve much the same purpose. Many
people find satisfaction, reward, fulfillment, and escape in a
hobby. A survey done at the Menninger Clinic some years ago indicated a positive relationship between significant involvement in
a hobby and good mental health.

It is a good idea to participate in a wide variety of recreational
activities. When children learn to play, they play alone at first.
Later they develop parallel play; that is, they play at things alone
but side by side. For example, they may each be swinging, playing
with toy cars, or building sand castles, but they are not interacting
with one another as part of the play. Still later, children begin to
play together, cooperating and interacting in their play. As adults,
we can use all of these types of play. We may want a hobby or some

form of recreation to do alone; in addition, we may want to read or paint or pursue some similar activity while family members or friends do something parallel. At other times, we may want to interact and cooperate, as in playing cards, chess, and so on. This satisfies the need for a variety of experiences in life.

As you begin to have more fun, you will find that you are more relaxed and less anxious. Periodic escape from everyday problems refreshes us and allows us to see the problems of living in perspective. Many people are so indoctrinated in the work ethic that they are unable to play or relax until they have first finished all their work. Of course, this is a trap, because we never finish all our work. Consequently, we never have occasion to play. A good way to handle this is to develop *work-play contingencies*. To do this, you need to specify a given task or portion of it that must be done. You then say to yourself, "When I finish that I will be entitled to a few hours of play for recreation and refreshment." You can then do the job and go play golf, go to a movie, or whatever you wish. Making play contingent on completing the work is good for a couple of reasons. First, it motivates you to get the work done more quickly, and you will be happier as you do it because you know that you are getting closer and closer to your recreation time. Second, you can enjoy the play without feeling guilty, because it is a reward for having done a significant job, which is now completed.

Putting work and play in this type of juxtaposition makes for a productive and happy lifestyle. Of course, you should also practice self-reinforcement at these times. Say to yourself, "That's good. I got the job done. I'm glad I did it. Now I'm going to go play golf. I'll get to that other job first thing tomorrow when I'm fresh and relaxed. It will go better then."

Be sure you don't set your goals too high. Some people pick a job that is too big to accomplish and still have enough time left over for play. The result, of course, is that they never quite get around to playing. If that is your problem, schedule a certain number of play hours after a specified number of hours of work rather than after completion of the job. You can say, "I'm going to work

Periodic escape from everyday problems refreshes us and allows us to see the problems of living in perspective.

on the yard for four hours in the morning on Saturday. Then, I'm going to relax and watch the ball game on TV. What I don't get done in that four hours, I'll do next Saturday. But I'm really going to work hard during those four hours." If you do this, you will find that Parkinson's Law (work will expand or contract to fill the time provided to do it) often applies to this type of situation. If you have three or four things to do in the yard and have set no time limit, they may take all day. But if you set a 4-hour time limit, you will generally get all or most of the work done in that amount of time, if you really try. Then you will have 4 hours for relaxation, and you've still accomplished the same amount of work.

If you are determined to have fun in life, often you can approach work playfully and enjoy it more than you otherwise might.

One final word: If you are determined to have fun in life, often you can approach work playfully and enjoy it more than you otherwise might. Suppose you have a boring task to do—perhaps peeling apples for a pie. If two people work at it, each can take an equal number of apples and race to see who finishes first. The loser has to peel the remaining apples or clean up the mess afterward. This is, of course, a very simple example, but the point is that if you make an effort and use a little creativity, a lot of things in life can be approached playfully and enjoyed rather than merely endured. Such an approach to work and play is an antidote to much of the anxiety we experience daily.

STRESS MANAGEMENT EXERCISES

1. Do you stay in a rut of fear or anxiety because it has become a habit and it is comfortable? Write about your thoughts on this. If it is true, make a resolution to break out of that rut.

_____

_____

_____

_____

_____

_____

_____

_____

_____

_____

_____

_____

_____

_____

_____

_____

2. Do you think you are a workaholic? Write your answer and give your reasons for it.

_____

_____

_____

_____

_____

_____

_____

_____

_____

_____

_____

_____

_____

_____

3. Ask your spouse or a friend to decide if he or she thinks you are a workaholic. Have the person write what he or she thinks in the following space.

_____

_____

_____

_____

_____

_____

_____

_____

_____

_____

_____

_____

_____

_____

_____

_____

_____

_____

_____

_____

_____

_____

_____

_____

4. If you are a workaholic, discuss with your spouse or friend a plan to reduce this problem in your life and write out your plan.

_____

_____

_____

_____

_____

_____

_____

_____

_____

_____

_____

_____

_____

_____

_____

_____

5. Analyze your schedule for times when you need a tactical retreat. Do you need one at noon (at work), in the evening (at home), on Sunday afternoon, or when? Think of something you can do to reduce the pressure at that time. Make that part of your regular routine or schedule. Write about your plan.

_____

_____

_____

_____

_____

_____

_____

_____

_____

_____

6. List five activities that you like to do alone for recreation and escape. Plan some time to do one or more of them each week for the next month. If you enjoy them, do them again the next month.

_____

_____

_____

_____

_____

_____

_____

_____

_____

7. List five activities that you like to do with others for recreation and escape. Pick one or two of them. Contact some friends and arrange to do those things together in the next month. If it is fun, do it again.

_____

_____

_____

_____

_____

_____

_____

_____

_____

_____

8. List three hobbies you have thought you might enjoy, but have never tried. Through the library, or by attending meetings of individuals who participate in the hobbies you have listed, find out more about the hobby and decide if you would like to adopt the hobby for yourself.

_____
_____
_____
_____
_____
_____
_____
_____
_____

9. Pick a job you have to do and develop a work-play plan as described on page 179 to accomplish the task. Write down your thoughts about how this worked.

_____
_____
_____
_____
_____
_____
_____
_____
_____
_____
_____
_____
_____
_____
_____

_____

_____

_____

_____

_____

_____

_____

_____

10. Pick a big job that you have been putting off until you have time to do all of it and schedule 3 or 4 hours to work on the job as described on page 208. Break the job into different phases, if possible. Write your reaction to how this worked. Make plans for additional work sessions until the job is complete.

_____

_____

_____

_____

_____

_____

_____

_____

_____

_____

_____

_____

_____

I 2

Friends and Communication

HUMAN BEINGS FIND considerable support and comfort in close relationships with others. The poet John Donne put it so well that his words have been quoted over and over:

> No man is an island, entire of itself; every man is a piece of the continent, a part of the main; if a clod be washed away by the sea, Europe is the less, as well as if a promontory were, as well as if a manor of thy friends or of thine own were; any man's death diminishes me, because I am involved in mankind; and therefore never send to know for whom the bell tolls; it tolls for thee.

Having friends and being able to communicate meaningfully with them is a great bulwark against anxiety. It used to be that the immediate and extended families (aunts, uncles, grandparents, cousins, etc.) gave stability to people's lives and offered support in times of crisis. The extended family gave the individual a context in which to view himself or herself. There were frequent family gatherings with stories about family history and what various relatives had done and were doing. There was security in knowing

Having friends and being able to communicate meaningfully with them is a great bulwark against anxiety.

that one was not alone, that people cared and could be called upon for help in times of crisis such as birth, death, illness, and financial problems. There were no questions asked—it was family. People did what had to be done to see one another through.

More recently, however, with the increased mobility of society, the increasing tempos of our lives, and the breakdown of the nuclear family, "the family" per se is no longer able to fulfill such needs. Members are scattered all over the country. They are busy with their own lives, and distance prevents them from developing a feeling of attachment to the others. The expense and disruption involved in coming to the aid of a cousin or a brother often seem too great a sacrifice. Many young people deliberately arrange their lives so that they can be away from their families and on their own. As someone has said, "Fate provides us with family, but we can choose our friends and associates." Yet, facing crises without family can be very stressful and anxiety provoking.

For many people, friends take the place of the extended family. There are, of course, different levels of friendship. Most of us know a fairly large number of people who are friends in the sense that we recognize one another and carry on conversations when we happen to meet. There are other friends whom we enjoy being around sufficiently that we seek out occasions when we can meet. There are still other friends to whom we feel very close, with whom we share important aspects of our lives and on whom we can call anytime we are in need.

Unfortunately, many people have trouble making friends, but there are some rules that can help in making friends and keeping them. First, as is often pointed out, the best way to have a friend is to be a friend—an interesting turn of phrase, but it is important to understand what it means. It means that if you want to have friends, you need to do the things that make friends of people. When you meet people, you need to come out of your shell and become interested in them and their worlds. Often we are so preoccupied with our worlds and so concerned about whether we will make a good impression that we never really make contact

The best way to have a friend is to be a friend.

with an individual we have just met. It is important to forget ourselves and reach out to others when we meet them. Try to find out who they are and what they are interested in. Remember, a stranger is just a friend you haven't met yet. Once you find out a little about someone, you can share some of your thoughts and experiences with that person. It also helps to smile a little and express pleasure about something the person says.

A second rule is that to develop friendships, you must develop a great deal of acceptance and patience. You must accept people as they are and not expect them to try to change to suit you. Psychiatrist Fritz Perls put it very well when he said of others that they were not here to measure up to his expectations, nor he to theirs. He went on to say that we are to do our own thing and be ourselves. If we develop a relationship in the process, that is wonderful; if not, it cannot be helped. Of course, as a person gets to know and associate with us, he or she may change, but that must not be one of the conditions of friendship. Good friendship develops out of a certain amount of unconditional positive regard. When people do what we don't like, we could take offense, but it is necessary to overlook some things and forget them. We have to realize that people are that way. They are not perfect. Because we're not perfect either, they will have to overlook our shortcomings.

As friendship develops, you can strengthen and enhance it by doing small favors and showing little kindnesses to the person. Being able to accept similar favors from others graciously is the other side of the coin. Some people are quite willing to do things for others but cannot bring themselves to let anyone do something for them; it's important to develop the ability both to give *and* to receive.

Two further points should be kept in mind. One is that to make friends, you have to come in contact with people who are potential friends. You can't sit at home and expect them to come and find you. There are numerous ways to come in contact with potential friends. You can invite people to your home for dinner, parties, or get-togethers. You can go to places where you'll meet people: churches, civic clubs, hobby groups, discussion groups, and so on. If you get involved in community and social activities, you'll make friends of some of the people you come in contact with.

The second point is that it is seldom possible to force friendship on someone; friendship is a lot like a love relationship in that sense. Some people will like you, and a friendship will develop. Others, for a variety of reasons, will not, and a friendship will not develop. Real friendship has to be something that clicks between people. It can't be forced and doesn't work if it is one-sided. You need to spend your time and energy selecting and developing friends from those who are interested, rather than lamenting the fact that some people with whom you'd like to be friendly don't seem interested.

Psychologists frequently refer to friendship as being based on patterns of mutual reinforcement. Essentially, this means that if the way a person looks, acts, thinks, and believes is pleasing to us, we'll want to spend more time in that person's company. We say that being with this individual is fun. It is reinforcing and rewarding to us. If that person feels the same way about us, a friendship develops. This principle explains a lot of things about friendship. For example, friendships change over the years. We may no longer enjoy being with people we once liked, and people we once had little time for may come to be our closest friends. If we analyze what has happened, we may find that our interests, needs, and style of living have changed over the years, so that the type of person whose behavior is rewarding to us has changed.

The principle of mutual reinforcement also explains why close friends can become bitter enemies (the line between love and hate is very thin). If our association with a person leads to mutual reinforcement, we become friends. If this person begins to thwart us in achieving or enjoying some important reward, however, we can become just as angry with the person as we were friendly before.

One of the best features of having friends is communication.

Humans are the only animals that communicate by means of highly complex language and symbol systems. Hours spent in conversation with close friends are stimulating, rewarding, and anxiety-reducing. Getting something off our chest by telling a friend about it makes us feel much better. Frequently friends are able to extend support or share some of their experiences with us. This can make a difference. Many times simply putting our thoughts into words clarifies our thinking and cuts through the nebulous quality of what is troubling us. When we clarify our thoughts and feelings, sometimes they seem to be less frightening. They seemed worse than they really were mainly because we had not pinned them down and looked at them objectively.

Hours spent in conversation with close friends are stimulating, rewarding, and anxiety-reducing.

Good communication between friends demands trust between the two. We need to feel free to tell our friends what we want to say. We need to be able to trust the friend to handle the information we give. Some people will be ruled out of this depth of friendship, but those we include will be people of special importance. Actually, a tragedy of many people's lives is that they often overlook the fact that a husband or a wife can be a best friend. That person is, after all, one who cares and is deeply involved with them for better or for worse. We may need to communicate with and cultivate our partners as best friends. Strange to say, most marriage relationships exist on a more superficial and defensive level than this.

While we need to have trust in our friends, we also need to have empathy for each other. *Empathy* is the ability to understand and fully appreciate how a person feels while remaining objective about it. It is different from sympathy. In sympathy one feels the same emotion as the other person and becomes involved in the same experience as the other. This reduces the ability to be objective and to help the person effectively. For example, if someone is depressed about something and you sympathize with that person, you begin to become depressed also. At that point, you both feel bad, and you are not able to help much. If you were feeling empathy, however, you would fully appreciate how the person really

Empathy is the ability to understand and fully appreciate how a person feels while remaining objective about it.

felt but would maintain enough objectivity to perceive the situation accurately. You would then be able to see workable solutions and go about putting them into operation. The result of empathy is the ability to help.

Communication involves two processes: talking and listening. People may have trouble with either or both. Some people have trouble talking. They find it difficult to put their ideas and feelings into words. Many times they don't know the right words to use; other times, they know the words but are afraid to say them for fear they will get an unpleasant response. If you have trouble talking, you need first to find a friend you trust and who has the ability to empathize with you. Then you must force yourself to talk to that person about your thoughts and feelings. You may start out with little things and short conversations, if you wish, and build up to more important and more extensive conversations later— but you must begin to talk. Not even friends can read your mind.

Some people who find it difficult to talk write letters and notes to others when the occasion arises. Often they can express their deeper feelings much more accurately this way. It is easy to do this by writing a note on a birthday, holiday, or anniversary card, or one of the many cards designed just to say thanks or to send a brief thought to a person. In addition, you can write to others when you or they are out of town, or during vacations. A friend of mine used to write notes to her husband and put them in with his lunch. He really looked forward to reading her notes while he ate. It gave both him and her a great lift each day.

The other side of communication is listening. We need to learn to listen to what people say to us. Sometimes this means just being quiet long enough for them to say what they want to. Often we have a tendency to interrupt or to jump to conclusions before the other person has finished talking. It is an art worth developing to be able to hear people out and let them say, in their own words, what they want to say. Of course you also need to be sure that you really understand what they mean. Take in and carefully analyze what they are saying. Try to forget your own preconceptions and see things through their eyes and their value systems so that you can really understand. It does no good to apply your own value system to the situation and discard as unimportant facts or details that the other person considers very important. When you are not sure just how a person thinks or feels about something, try saying something like, "I'm not sure I follow, but what you seem to be saying is this. . . ." Then repeat the sense of what the other person said, as best you can interpret it. This technique gives the other person the opportunity to agree with or correct your statement.

Sometimes it is important to go behind the words another person is saying and tune in to the underlying feelings. Tone of voice, physical posture, and gesture may all reveal anxiety, frustration, anger, joy, and other emotions that are not obvious from the words being used in the conversation. Generally if you pay attention to these cues you will communicate and understand much better. If you are pretty sure of the message coming from these cues, you can respond to the content of the words and the subtle cues without necessarily labeling them and making a major point of letting the person know you have picked them up. This often elicits a feeling of warmth and friendship that says, "You understand me. I know you do. Thanks." You do have to be sure you have correctly interpreted those cues, or you may eventually run into a blank wall or lose contact with the person. If you seem to be headed in that direction, it is often helpful to stop and say something like, "I'm not sure I fully understand. Do you seem to feel this way?" You can then label the feeling you think you picked up from the cues. The other person, again, can agree with or correct your impression.

In all relationships, it is possible for conflict or disagreement to develop. These situations can produce anxiety. One good way to resolve conflict is for the two people to stop before a bitter argument develops and do an exercise in which each takes the role of the other person. Thus, with a married couple, the husband would argue his wife's side of the issue as persuasively as possible, as though he were her attorney or representative. His case for her

One good way to resolve conflict is for the two people to stop before a bitter argument develops and do an exercise in which each takes the role of the other person.

side should include her feelings, views, arguments, reasons, and so forth. He should go beyond what she has actually said and add to her side. Following this, she should respond with clarification on points where he may have been inaccurate. She would then present his side of the issue, and he would provide clarification. This exercise almost always reduces the anger and promotes communication. The next step is to brainstorm (see Chapter 9) for solutions.

Relationships based on positive regard, patience, trust, empathy, and effective conflict resolution are true and lasting friendships that comfort us in times of crisis and serve as bulwarks against many of the stresses of life. Clinical psychologist Carl Rogers studied and wrote extensively about such relationships. Many of his books are helpful, especially *On Becoming a Person, Person to Person,* and *Becoming Partners: Marriage and Its Alternatives.*

A psychiatrist friend of mine developed a personal audit system that he uses as a part of his everyday routine. One part of it involves making a list of people who are important to him, such as his parents, wife, children, close friends and so forth. Each day he reads that list and asks himself, "What does [the person's name] need from me today?" He then plans his activities for the day. The personal audit may lead him to plan to call his parents, thank his wife for something she did, attend a school activity for one of his children, and say "Happy Birthday" to a friend. Having the list and reviewing it each day keeps relationships current and reduces the likelihood of overlooking important needs of those we care about. It also helps one keep perspective on the things that really matter in life.

STRESS MANAGEMENT EXERCISES

1. In the space following, list the individuals to whom you can turn in times of stress. Make separate lists for immediate family, extended family, close friends, and others.

_____

_____

_____

_____

_____

_____

_____

_____

_____

_____

_____

_____

_____

_____

_____

_____

_____

_____

_____

_____

_____

_____

_____

2. Are there enough people on your list? Are there categories where additional people would be helpful? How can you add to your list?

_____

_____

_____

_____

_____

_____

_____

_____

_____

_____

_____

_____

3. List the names of some individuals with whom you would like to develop a friendship. Using the ideas presented on pages 188–191 develop a plan to initiate a friendship with each of the people on the list.

_____

_____

_____

_____

_____

_____

_____

_____

_____

_____

_____

_____

_____

_____

_____

_____

_____

_____

4. Ask a friend to give you some feedback on whether you are a good listener and conversationalist. Using the techniques described in this chapter, practice improving communication between the two of you. Write about your experience and list the areas that need more work.

_____

_____

_____

_____

_____

_____

_____

_____

_____

_____

_____

_____

_____

_____

_____

5. Observe a person who is good at small talk and use that person as a model to develop better skills in this area. Write down the techniques that seem to work best for you.

_____

_____

_____

_____

_____

_____

_____

_____

_____

_____

_____

_____

6. Pick a person with whom you need to communicate regarding a difficult situation (an unresolved conflict, misunderstanding, or something similar) and write that person a letter or select a suitable card on which to send a note in order to effect a reconciliation. Write the outcome in the space following. Are there other people with whom you need to do the same thing?

_____

_____

_____

_____

_____

_____

_____

_____

_____

_____

_____

_____

_____

_____

_____

_____

_____

_____

_____

_____

7. Use the perspective-taking technique (in which you argue the other person's case and he or she argues yours) described on pages 193–194 to resolve a problem with a family member or friend. Write about the results.

_____

_____

_____

_____

_____

_____

_____

_____

_____

_____

_____

_____

8. Make a list of the most important people in your life. Begin a program in which you review your list each morning to think about what each of these people needs from you. Plan your day so that you can respond to these needs. Write your list in the following space and jot down some of your thoughts as you follow through with your program.

_____

_____

_____

_____

_____

_____

_____

_____

_____

_____

_____

_____

_____

_____

_____

_____

_____

_____

_____

_____

_____

_____

13

Self-Hypnosis

HYPNOSIS IS A CONTROVERSIAL area. Over the years the popularity of hypnosis in psychological treatment has waxed and waned. It has, from time to time, received wide attention and endorsement as a legitimate and useful therapeutic tool, only to fall into disrepute and disuse with the next generation of psychotherapists. There is currently considerable interest in hypnosis as a tool of treatment, and research is going on in many important research centers that will enable us to understand the phenomenon better and use it effectively in therapy.

Hypnosis falls out of favor with therapists for two main reasons. One is that it has often been offered as a panacea for all kinds of problems. When it becomes apparent, after some scrutiny, that hypnosis is not a cure-all, many therapists seem to lose interest. The second reason is that we have never really established just what hypnosis is. Lacking a full understanding of its nature, many psychologists are reluctant to use it.

Some assert that hypnosis is an altered state of consciousness. They claim that a hypnotized person is in a trance, which gives that person the ability to draw on the subconscious or to alter brain chemistry and functioning. At the other extreme are people who

Over the years the popularity of hypnosis in psychological treatment has waxed and waned.

say there is no such thing as hypnosis. They say the subject is just role-playing and responding to the suggestions of the hypnotist. The nay-sayers have conducted research in the area and have been able to demonstrate that they can get their research subjects to do most, if not all, of the things hypnotized subjects do but without ever having been hypnotized. The subjects simply try hard and are as cooperative as possible.

Before we present an overview of what hypnosis is, it is important to be clear about what it is not. There is hardly an area of psychology that is riddled with as many misconceptions as hypnosis. First, hypnosis is not a form of sleep. Extensive studies of bodily reactions of the waking, hypnotic, and sleep states have demonstrated that hypnosis isn't sleep, even though hypnotists often use the phrase "You are going to sleep" as part of the hypnotic induction procedure. Hypnosis is closer to a waking state than to sleep, but it is not identical with being awake either.

Second, the experience of hypnosis is generally not a weird, mysterious, otherworldly experience. Many stage hypnotists who perform mainly for entertainment play up this notion and encourage their subjects to feel that way. This is not an intrinsic part of the process, however, and it seldom occurs when hypnosis is used in psychotherapy. It is a very normal, interesting, but unspectacular experience for most people. In fact, many times when I use it with patients, they require reassurance afterward that they were really hypnotized before they will believe it. The experience lacked the supernatural quality that they'd expected it to have. By conducting certain tests of their reactions during the process, however, it is possible to verify that they were indeed hypnotized.

Third, a person who is hypnotized is not under the power of the hypnotist. The hypnotized person does not surrender his or her will or lose control of his or her own behavior. The person does become more susceptible to suggestion but only to the extent that he or she wishes to be. If the hypnotist suggests that the person do something to which he or she has no strong objections, the person probably will do it; but if the hypnotist suggests something that the person really doesn't want to do, he or she simply won't do it. People are sometimes concerned that a hypnotist will take advantage of a subject and get him or her to do something antisocial or criminal. This is not possible if the person really doesn't want to do it. It is possible, however, to get people to do such things with or without hypnosis if they want to or can be persuaded to do it. Hypnotism has not been found to increase persuasibility toward this kind of behavior very much, if at all. In any case, a responsible hypnotist would not even suggest such a thing. Thus, reports of hypnotism's use to involve people in crime or sexual activity are greatly exaggerated. Hypnotism isn't that powerful. As a precaution against even the remote possibility, however, it is wise to deal only with a fully trained and responsible hypnotist, such as a clinical psychologist, psychiatrist, or some other professional person.

It is wise to deal only with a fully trained and responsible hypnotist, such as a clinical psychologist, psychiatrist, or some other professional person.

Many people who think hypnotism has special power are disappointed when they ask me to hypnotize them and tell them that they won't smoke anymore, drink anymore, or eat so much. It simply doesn't work that way.

Another frequent misconception is that the subject will not remember anything about what went on during hypnosis after waking up. Actually, when the session is over the hypnotized person generally remembers everything that went on. The only time a person wouldn't remember would be when specific instructions are given by the hypnotist not to do so; this is referred to as *posthypnotic amnesia*. It occurs only when instructions to that effect are given or when the person firmly believes that such will be the effect, or both. Furthermore, instructions for posthypnotic amnesia don't always work. If you want to remember, you generally do. Posthypnotic amnesia is usually not called for in hypnotherapy but can be very useful on occasion. Often, if I'm working with a patient on matters that are quite upsetting, I will induce posthypnotic amnesia for a period of time during the treatment until we get some of the problems resolved and they are not so painful to think about. This makes the patient more comfortable between sessions. In all other cases, patients remember everything, which is best because it facilitates the treatment.

Some people worry that if they become hypnotized they may not be able to wake up. This never happens. Some people who are hypnotized resist releasing that state at the end, often because they have found relief and escape in the hypnotic state and don't want to let go of it. This is quite rare, however, and when it happens, the hypnotist can continue to work on bringing the patient out of it for a time. If that doesn't work, it is best to put the person in a comfortable place and wait. Generally, he or she will fall asleep and later wake up alert. Or, the person may rest in the hypnotic state for a while and then voluntarily come out of it. Nobody has gone into a hypnotic state and never come out.

Nobody has gone into a hypnotic state and never come out.

People often say they have tried but can't be hypnotized. Even some scientific literature claims a certain percentage of people cannot be hypnotized; it depends a lot on how one defines hypnosis. There are levels of hypnosis. Probably everyone, with the possible exception of some severely retarded or severely psychotic individuals, can achieve some degree of hypnosis, even if it is very slight.

All right. How can we define hypnosis? First, we have to keep in mind that there is no adequate and perfectly clear definition. We simply don't understand the process well enough to define or explain it fully. As a working definition for our purposes, though, it is useful to think of hypnosis as a heightened motivational state of concentration accompanied by an increased ability to act on ideas and suggestions. It is possible to think of a *distraction-concentration continuum.* At the extreme distraction end of the continuum people are woefully inefficient at performing even the simplest tasks. For example, if you had to walk across a stage, pour a glass of water, and give your name and address in front of an audience of 10,000 people, you probably would have great difficulty doing these simple tasks because of the distraction and anxiety caused by being the subject of the audience's observation. You might stumble across the stage (having forgotten how to walk), pour water on your wrist, throw the glass over your shoulder, and draw a blank on your name and address. At the other end of the continuum, when we are in deep concentration, we become highly efficient and can accomplish extremely challenging tasks. Our complete concentration and the fact that we are engrossed in the task make it easy for us.

Some people are able to get into this state of concentration easily. When they read a book or think about a problem, they shut out all extraneous stimuli from the environment. If you walk into the room and say something to them, they may not even hear you until you go over and shake them. These people are fast readers, good students, and good problem solvers. Other people are more easily distracted and less efficient in such tasks.

Examples of concentration are plentiful among athletes. For example, we often talk about a good baseball player being "off at the crack of the bat." When I played baseball, I was able to sprint for the ball very quickly and found that I could reach fly balls that nobody expected me to. I did it by concentrating on the ball while it was still in the pitcher's glove, following with deep concentration through the windup and the ball's flight to the plate. When the ball was hit, I was off at once. In actuality, I was in a type of hypnotic state. Basketball players who stare at the basket, bounce the ball a couple of times, and take a few deep breaths are getting into a similar state before they make a foul shot. When they get into that state, crowd noise and attempted distractions don't bother them. They are able to make the shot. Pass receivers in football require the same ability. If they try to run with the ball before they have caught it securely, they usually drop it. Their concentration has been lost. We often say when they drop a pass that they heard the footsteps behind them—another example of disrupted concentration.

If we view hypnosis as a state of deep concentration on selected stimuli, it is easy to see why we can act more readily on suggestions and carry out ideas more efficiently under hypnosis. This view is a useful working definition, regardless of whether it proves

Hypnosis *is a state of*
deep concentration on
selected stimuli.

to be the final answer to the riddle of hypnosis. Hypnosis then becomes a way of inducing deeper concentration in ourselves at will, so that we can efficiently carry out tasks we want to do.

There are countless ways to induce hypnosis. It is relatively easy for a skilled hypnotist to induce the state in a cooperative subject; it is also relatively easy for you to induce hypnosis in yourself. One simple way to do this is to hold your hand at arm's length in front of your face at eye level. Then stare at a point on the hand. It can be any point such as a knuckle, ring, or freckle. The important thing is focusing vision on one spot. Then move the hand slowly toward your forehead and bring the point on which you have focused up to the forehead, right between your eyes. When your hand touches your forehead, close your eyes, and go through the relaxation procedure outlined in Chapter 6. At this point you will be completely relaxed and your eyes will be closed. Now begin to count, and with each count let your body relax a little more and go a little deeper into the state of hypnosis. Beginners may want to count to 45 or 50. With a little practice you will be able to achieve satisfactory results by counting to only 10 or 15. At the end of this procedure you will be in a light state of hypnosis.

An alternate procedure is to roll the eyes back into the head as far as you can for a few seconds (rather than focusing on the hand and moving it to the forehead). Follow this with the same relaxation and counting procedure as above.

Once you achieve a light state of hypnosis, you can use it to relieve anxiety. One way is simply to tell yourself that you are going to calm down and get things under control. You will often find that this works wonders. When you leave the hypnotic state you will feel much better, less tense, and more relaxed.

You can think through
problems in this state
and figure out ways to
handle them.

You can also think through problems in this state and figure out ways to handle them. The relaxation and freedom from distraction will facilitate good problem solving. In this state you can also tell yourself things that you know are true and would like to accept emotionally, but of which you have not been able to convince yourself while awake. Hypnosis will make you more able to respond to such ideas or suggestions. For example, you might say to yourself, "I'm going to interview for that job next week. There is no need to be overly anxious about it. It is normal to be a little tense in such a situation, and I'll be that. But I'll be more relaxed than I have in similar situations before. After all, the interview isn't that important. If I get the job, fine. If not, there is no sense in being anxious about it. Being calm will actually enhance my chances and make me more likely to handle the interview well and get the job. I'll be very calm. If I don't get it, maybe next time." Under hypnosis you can talk to yourself and tell yourself things of this sort. They will have a greater impact and be more believable. It's amazingly simple, but it works.

Some people also like to think about pleasant or calm situations and experiences under hypnosis. This is very similar to the meditation exercises discussed in Chapter 6. There is great similarity between hypnosis and meditation. In fact, many of the feats of the Yogis and other mystics are probably attributable to a type of hypnotic process.

After you have used hypnosis to help reduce your anxiety, it is simple to wake up (we'll use that term here for convenience, although, as we've discussed, you are not in any way asleep). You simply say, "I am now going to wake up. I will feel refreshed, relaxed, and wide awake. My mind will be clear, and I will feel good all over." Then open your eyes. You will feel as if you have just awakened from a nap or stopped working on something that completely engrossed your interest. It is a pleasant and exhilarating experience.

A word of caution is called for here: If hypnosis seems frightening to you or you are unsure of it, don't do it. It should be a pleasant, helpful experience. If the very idea of it frightens you, or if it seems to have that effect once you try it, stop. Under such circumstances, it is best to consult a professionally trained hypnotist before going on. The professional may work with you and help you get over your fear, or may tell you that hypnosis is not for you at this time. If you have tried self-hypnosis and it didn't seem to work

Hypnosis should be a pleasant, helpful experience.

very well, it is also best to consult a professionally trained person. To find a qualified professional hypnotist, call the chairman of the psychology department at a nearby college or the head of the psychiatry department of a nearby medical school and ask him or her for a referral.

STRESS MANAGEMENT EXERCISES

1. Have you experienced some of the heightened states of concentration that are a form of natural hypnotic experience? If so, write about them in the following space.

_____

_____

_____

_____

_____

_____

_____

_____

_____

_____

_____

_____

_____

_____

_____

_____

_____

_____

_____

_____

2. Have you ever been hypnotized by another person? Describe your experience. Do you find it easy or difficult to enter into a hypnotic state?

_____

_____

_____

_____

_____

_____

_____

_____

_____

_____

_____

_____

_____

_____

_____

_____

_____

_____

_____

_____

_____

_____

_____

_____

_____

_____

_____

3. Pick a time early in the day and use the technique described on page 206 in which you stare at your hand to induce hypnosis. After you are hypnotized, just relax and say to yourself, "I am peaceful. I am calm." Do this for a few minutes. Then say, "I am going to awaken at the count of three and I will feel fully relaxed and refreshed. I will be optimistic and full of energy for the rest of the day." Write down how you felt during and after this exercise.

_____

_____

_____

_____

_____

_____

_____

_____

_____

_____

_____

_____

_____

_____

_____

_____

_____

_____

_____

_____

_____

_____

_____

4. Choose a problem that you want to work on and use the hypnotic induction technique described on page 206, in which you roll your eyes back in your head. Think through your problem and come up with a solution. Then, tell yourself to act on the solution when you end the hypnotic session. Write down your problem and the solution. Later, write about whether you found it easy to act on the solution developed under hypnosis.

_____

_____

_____

_____

_____

_____

_____

_____

_____

_____

_____

_____

_____

_____

_____

_____

_____

_____

_____

_____

_____

_____

_____

5. Use either of the techniques for hypnotic induction and then repeat to yourself some positive self-statements that you want to incorporate into your life (e.g., If I do my best at work, I will have success and I am up to the job; I don't have to be perfect or always make the right decision, I just have to do the best I can; I will do what I think is right even if it does not make me popular—in the long run, others will understand). Write the statements you have chosen here. Did hypnosis help you incorporate these ideas into your thoughts and life?

_____

_____

_____

_____

_____

_____

_____

_____

_____

_____

_____

_____

_____

_____

_____

_____

_____

_____

_____

_____

6. Use the technique of rolling your eyes back in your head to induce hypnosis while lying in bed. Then, repeat some of your positive self-statements from Exercise 5 and go through a relaxation exercise from Chapter 6. Next day, write how you felt when you awakened and how the day went.

_____

_____

_____

_____

_____

_____

_____

_____

_____

_____

_____

_____

_____

_____

_____

_____

_____

_____

_____

_____

_____

_____

_____

7. Use the hypnotic induction techniques over the next 2 months. Each time you use them, evaluate yourself on how well you were able to achieve the hypnotic state and record your score (grade yourself on a scale of 0 to 100, with 0 being completely unsuccessful and 100 being completely successful) as well as your thoughts and observations. Over time, your score should improve. If it does not or is below 60, you might want to consult a mental health professional who is trained in the use of hypnosis. Contact the chair of the psychology department of a nearby college for a referral.

_____

_____

_____

_____

_____

_____

_____

_____

_____

_____

_____

_____

_____

_____

_____

_____

_____

_____

_____

_____

_____

14

Professional Help

AFTER READING THIS BOOK and trying some of the techniques that seem to fit your situation best, you may find that you are still experiencing more stress and anxiety than you would like. You want to be calmer about things and relaxed enough to enjoy life rather than having it be such a struggle. Sometimes your anxiety may be related to a specific situation that will change after a short period of time; if this is the case, it may be best just to wait it out, much as you would a cold or similar minor ailment. Everyone has short periods of stress and anxiety from time to time that must be endured just as other unpleasant things in life must be. But if your anxiety is persistent, it may be best for you to seek help from a professional psychotherapist. Your problems may be such that they need more help than can be offered in a book like this. Or you may just need a little help from someone with more experience in carrying out the techniques outlined in this book. In any event, if you decide to seek professional help, here are some points worth considering.

The first place most people go with this type of problem is to their family physician or minister. While the family physician or minister can be helpful, especially if the anxiety is relatively mi-

If your anxiety is persistent, it may be best for you to seek help from a professional psychotherapist.

nor and not related to more serious problems, this may not be the best choice. The physician has had little or no training in psychotherapy but can offer reassurance and advice based on the wisdom grown out of involvement with many people's lives. A physician can also prescribe medications that will reduce the discomfort you may be experiencing. These medications will be discussed in more detail later in this chapter. Some ministers are trained in counseling and can be quite helpful; others lack training or skills in this area. The important thing to keep in mind is that the family physician and the minister are prepared to help with only minor, short-term anxiety problems. Their major training and skills lie in other areas.

For people with more serious anxiety problems, the best source of help is generally a clinical psychologist, a psychiatrist, a social worker, or a licensed counselor. Numerous surveys have shown that most people are uncertain about what difference there is among these.

A *clinical psychologist* is a person who has earned a doctoral degree in psychology, with specialization in the areas of psychopathology, diagnostic evaluation, treatment of people with emotional disturbances, and related areas. This degree requires approximately 10 years of academic training, including 4 years of undergraduate training in psychology, at least 4 or more years of graduate training in psychology, and thousands of hours of practical training and experience. During the graduate training, in addition to relevant courses, the clinical psychologist works in treatment settings such as hospitals and clinics under the supervision of more experienced psychologists. He or she then completes a year of internship and undergoes an additional year or more of supervision after the doctoral degree is awarded. At this point, the person may be licensed to offer services on an independent basis to the public. The clinical psychologist is trained and experienced in the basic sciences pertaining to the diagnosis and treatment of emotional disturbances.

The *psychiatrist* is a physician who has decided to specialize in the treatment of people suffering from emotional disturbances. The psychiatrist, therefore, completes 3 or 4 years of undergraduate study, 3 or 4 years of medical school, and, generally, a 3- or 4-year psychiatry residency. As a resident the psychiatrist serves on the staff of a hospital or clinic and receives additional training and supervision in the treatment of emotional disturbances.

In terms of the rigor and extensiveness of their respective kinds of training, clinical psychologists and psychiatrists have essentially equivalent backgrounds. Both training programs are highly competitive, require a high degree of ability and diligence to complete, and take about the same number of years. The main difference is that one produces a psychologist who has decided to specialize in the treatment of emotionally disturbed individuals rather than one of the other areas of psychology, while the other produces a physician who has decided to specialize in the treatment of the emotionally disturbed rather than in one of the other areas of medicine. In most of their routine clinical practices, psychologists and psychiatrists function similarly; but because their backgrounds are different, they do bring different skills to a situation. The physician is highly trained in the physical functioning of the body and is licensed to prescribe drugs. The psychologist is more highly trained in psychological functioning, personality theory, psychological diagnostic testing, and research. In many settings psychologists and psychiatrists work in teams to capitalize on the unique skills of each. In independent private practice, they generally develop cooperative relationships to accomplish the same thing. For example, if a psychiatrist has a difficult diagnostic decision to make, he or she frequently will refer the patient to a psychologist for an extensive personality evaluation using psychological tests before the diagnosis is made. Likewise, if a patient of a psychologist has a physical problem or needs medication, the psychologist will have a physician see the patient and attend to this aspect. There is currently considerable interest among some psychologists in obtaining necessary training and licensure to prescribe medications. Some have already achieved this; however,

Both clinical psychologists and psychiatrists offer excellent help for the emotionally disturbed.

most clinical psychologists do not prescribe. Both clinical psychologists and psychiatrists offer excellent help for the emotionally disturbed.

Social workers are also highly trained and very effective providers of mental health care. To become a social worker one must complete 4 years of undergraduate training and two years of graduate training in social work, leading to a Master of Social Work (MSW) degree. While it is possible to get a doctoral degree in social work, the MSW is considered the terminal degree for clinical practice. The doctoral degree is more for research and academic social workers. During graduate training, social workers receive extensive supervision in clinical work. To be licensed, they generally must be supervised for 2 years following completion of the MSW degree. A fully trained social worker should be licensed by the state to practice and be a member of the Academy of Certified Social Workers (ACSW). Social workers are trained to evaluate and treat emotional problems, including anxiety. Because their field has its roots in sociology, they often see cases in which family therapy or marital counseling is required (psychologists and psychiatrists also see patients for this type of treatment).

Recently many states have begun to license counselors who are trained to offer certain types of treatment in selected areas such as personal development or marriage and family problems. Generally, these therapists have a master's degree in some area of counseling, though some have a doctoral degree. They typically have 2 years of supervision in treatment before they are licensed. Licensed professional counselors can be very helpful in the areas in which they have been trained.

Another type of practitioner is the psychoanalyst. A psychoanalyst is a professionally trained person (usually a clinical psychologist or psychiatrist) who has had additional training and experience in the application of Freudian theory to the treatment of emotional disturbance. This usually involves 2 or 3 additional years of training as well as undergoing a personal psychoanalysis. Psychoanalysis generally requires several meetings a week for several years. Each session costs from $100 to $200, depending on the going rate in the area, the eminence of the therapist, and the patient's ability to pay. Due to the time and expense involved in psychoanalysis, it is generally not indicated except for serious problems. In recent years the efficacy and efficiency of psychoanalytic treatment has come under serious question. Many psychologists and psychiatrists feel that the beneficial results are not sufficient to justify the time and expense required.

One approach that is very useful in treating anxiety is called *behavior therapy*. It has been developed primarily in the last 30 or 40 years and draws heavily on research from psychological laboratories throughout the world. Numerous investigations have demonstrated that behavioral treatments work effectively and in a relatively short period of time to bring relief from many types of emotional disturbance. Many of the ideas presented in this book are based on behavior therapy techniques.

Once you have decided to see a professional psychotherapist, the problem becomes one of choosing the person you want to see. You can look in the yellow pages of the phone book, or ask friends to recommend someone they know. You may also want to check with the local psychological, medical, or social work societies for names. There are also state psychological, medical, and social work associations. A little inquiry and some help from the telephone information operator will help you locate their offices.

Once you have decided to see a professional psychotherapist, the problem becomes one of choosing the person you want to see.

Another good way to look for a suitable professional psychotherapist is to write or call the chair of the psychology or social work department of a nearby college or university or the department of psychiatry at a nearby medical school. Tell the person you contact the general nature of your problem and the type of psychotherapist you would like to see. They are generally quite willing to help.

As noted earlier in this chapter, certain types of medication are used to reduce anxiety. There are two major types of medication generally prescribed by physicians in such cases: sedatives and tranquilizers. Most sedatives are chemically benzodiazepines and have the effect of inhibiting and depressing the activity of the central nervous system (brain and spinal cord). They generally make a person feel calm. Some of the better-known brand names of these drugs are Librium, Valium, Serax, and Xanax.

Although sedatives technically are defined by their sedating effect on the central nervous system, they are often loosely referred to as tranquilizers or minor tranquilizers. Most of the real tranquilizers or major tranquilizers are chemically phenothiazine derivatives. Commonly known brand names of these are Thorazine, Mellaril, Stelazine, Trilafon, and Prolixin. How these drugs work is not completely understood, but they seem to affect centers of the brain that are involved in expressing emotional behavior. When the emotion-mediating centers of the brain are better controlled, the person feels more tranquil and less confused.

BuSpar is a medication that appears to be very effective in reducing anxiety but does not fit in either of the two major categories. Chemically it is quite different (technically an azaspiro-decane-dione).

One additional medication that your doctor may employ is called a beta blocker. Popular brands of this are Inderal and Tenormin. Chemically, these are propranolol and atenolol hydrochlorides, respectively. They take effect by blocking and reducing the effects of adrenaline on the autonomic nervous system. Adrenaline is what keys us up in threatening situations.

Usually sedatives, or minor tranquilizers and Buspar, are used in cases of simple tension and anxiety. Major tranquilizers are used when the patient's agitation is accompanied by symptoms of thought disturbance; confusion; hostile or aggressive behavior; and other, more serious, forms of emotional disturbance such as psychosis. Beta blockers are better than the others for brief use in highly specific and infrequent stressful situations such as giving a major speech, getting married, taking an oral exam in graduate school, and so on. Since depression often accompanies anxiety and makes stressful situations more difficult to handle, your physician may want to have you take an antidepressant such as Prozac as a part of your treatment. It is best to trust your physician's judgment as to what is best for you at a given time.

Most people do not know that alcohol, as found in the traditional alcoholic beverages of beer, wine, and whiskey, is chemically a sedative drug. It has essentially the same effect as the drugs mentioned previously, which are prescribed by a physician. As we are well aware, in our culture alcohol is a greatly abused and overused drug, because it is a fast-acting, short-term sedative. Thus, the sedative effects of the drug occur very shortly after ingestion but also wear off before long. Therefore, to maintain the effect, one must drink more. The body habituates to such drugs, so eventually, larger and more frequent doses are required to get the same effect. At this rate a person is apt to find himself or herself addicted to alcohol. It's a familiar pattern. The important thing to keep in mind is that alcohol is a drug, specifically a sedative and one to which we can become addicted. Therefore, it is best not to use it as a self-medication. When we have anxieties and tensions, we should learn to handle them by using the techniques presented earlier in this book. If we need medication, we should see a physician, who can prescribe a safer medication that will work better. By using the medication under supervision, we can be assured that we are less likely to abuse the drug or become addicted. Taking alcoholic beverages to relieve anxiety is too dangerous. If taken at all, alcoholic beverages are best in moderate amounts with meals or on social occasions for added pleasure, rather than as desperate attempts to escape from pain and anxiety.

Another important point is that drugs frequently interact with one another when taken together. Many times two drugs that are safe and helpful if taken separately can become extremely potent and dangerous if taken together. Alcohol acts much this way with some of the sedatives and tranquilizers previously mentioned. If one takes a small dose of some of these medications and then drinks a few ounces of alcohol, the combined effect can cause the person to be dangerously slow in reactions, making driving, working, or other activities very hazardous. He or she may also

The important thing to keep in mind is that alcohol is a drug, specifically a sedative and one to which we can become addicted.

lose consciousness and in some cases even die as a result. Be very careful about mixing medications or taking them with alcohol. Ask your physician before you do.

One other form of self-medication should be mentioned. Various patented medicines on the market are available in drugstores without a prescription. They are sold to relieve tension and to aid in going to sleep. Most of these contain small doses of antihistamines, which are known to produce a sedative effect. Many of them also contain other mild sedative agents, small amounts of pain-relieving medications, and sometimes vitamins. If you are experiencing mild, fleeting tension and anxiety, these are certainly worth a try. They may help to make stronger measures unnecessary. Your druggist can help you select one. They are reasonably safe and very economical. Be sure to use them as directed on the package. They should be used only for brief periods of time. If the problem persists more than a week or two, consult your physician.

The medications discussed here are primarily palliative rather than curative. That is, they will make you feel a little better temporarily, but they do not cure or clear up the problem. If the anxiety is brief and infrequent, they can be very helpful; but if it persists or comes back too often, chances are you need psychotherapeutic treatment by a trained professional. The sooner you find one and begin to work on your problems, the sooner you will feel better. Psychotherapy for anxiety-related problems is essential because many of the medications can be addictive if used over long periods of time. When this occurs, the cure for anxiety can be worse than the disease.

Psychotherapy for anxiety-related problems is essential because many of the medications can be addictive if used over long periods of time.

One final point should be mentioned before we end this book. That is that many people who work diligently, alone or with professional help, at reducing anxiety often report that when the anxiety begins to go down, depression begins to increase. This occurs in only a small number of cases, and it should not be a matter of great concern. Usually what has happened is that the person has been so accustomed to living under great tension or pressure that a normal, anxiety-free state seems flat and drab. Then he or she gets depressed. Generally if one is patient the depression will leave. It helps to involve yourself in things you enjoy and begin to make life more interesting and exciting. The points made in Chapter 11 can be helpful in this regard. If the depression is severe or persistent, you should contact a professional psychotherapist.

It helps to involve yourself in things you enjoy and begin to make life more interesting and exciting.

Be cool.

STRESS MANAGEMENT EXERCISES

1. If, after trying the approaches described in this book, you have problems that still persist, you may want to consult a professional. Write the questions you would like to ask such a person.

_____

_____

_____

_____

_____

_____

_____

_____

_____

_____

_____

_____

_____

_____

_____

2. Choose one or more of the questions from Exercise 1 and decide who might best answer them. Often, it is a good strategy to start with a physical exam by your physician and to ask for a referral; however, if you are certain your concern would be best handled by a mental health professional, you might want to contact the chair of the psychology department in a nearby university for a referral. After you talk with a professional, write down the answers you received to your questions.

_____

_____

_____

_____

_____

_____

_____

_____

_____

_____

_____

_____

_____

_____

_____

_____

_____

_____

_____

_____

_____

_____

_____

_____

_____

_____

3. Is there a medication that you think might be helpful to you? If so, go to the library and read about it in some reference books. The librarian can help you locate these. Write your findings and any questions you have in the space below.

_____

_____

_____

_____

_____

_____

_____

_____

_____

_____

_____

_____

_____

_____

_____

_____

_____

_____

4. Make an appointment with your family physician or a psychiatrist to get the answer to your questions and discuss the medication to determine if it would be helpful to you. Write the answer to your questions and your conclusion in the following space.

_____

_____

_____

_____

_____

_____

_____

_____

_____

_____

_____

_____

_____

_____

_____

_____

_____

_____

_____

_____

_____

_____

_____

_____

_____

5. Are you using any over-the-counter medications or remedies, legal substances (e.g., alcohol, nicotine), or illegal substances regularly? Make an appointment with your physician to discuss these. If they are not safe for you, have the physician refer you to a suitable treatment program. Write down your findings and thoughts here.

_____

_____

_____

_____

_____

_____

_____

_____

_____

_____

_____

_____

_____

_____

_____

_____

_____

_____

_____

_____

_____

_____

_____

_____

_____

6. Outline a program for the future in which you will use the things you have learned from this book. Be specific. Make a list of things to do to implement your program.

_____
_____
_____
_____
_____
_____
_____
_____
_____
_____
_____
_____
_____
_____
_____
_____
_____
_____

Suggested Reading

Alberti, Robert E., and Michael L. Emmons. *Your Perfect Right: A Guide to Assertive Living.* 25th ed. San Louis Obispo, CA: Impact, 1995. 256 pp.

Beck, Aaron T. *Love is Never Enough: How You Can Overcome Misunderstandings, Resolve Conflicts, and Solve Relationship Problems Through Cognitive Therapy.* New York: HarperCollins, 1989. 432 pp.

Benson, Herbert H., and Miriam Z. Klipper. *The Relaxation Response.* New York: Avon, 1990. 222 pp.

Benson, Herbert H., and Eileen M. Stuart. *The Wellness Book: The Comprehensive Guide to Maintaining Health and Treating Stress Related Illness.* New York: Simon & Schuster, 1993. 512 pp.

Bourne, Edmund J. *Anxiety and Phobia Workbook.* 2nd ed. Oakland, CA: New Harbinger, 1995. 428 pp.

Budilovsky, Joan, and Eve Adamson. *The Complete Idiot's Guide to Meditation.* New York: Macmillan, 1999. 455 pp.

Burns, David D. *Ten Days to Self-Esteem.* New York: William Morrow & Co. Quill, 1999. 331 pp.

Burns, David D., and Aaron T. Beck. *Feeling Good: The New Mood Therapy.* New York: Avon, 1992. 466 pp.

Carlson, Richard. *Don't Sweat the Small Stuff—And It's All Small Stuff.* New York: Hyperion, 1997. 248 pp.

Culp, Stephanie. *You Can Find More Time for Yourself Every Day.* Cincinnati, OH: Betterway, 1994. 210 pp.

Davich, Victor N., and Jack Canfield. *The Best Guide to Meditation.* Los Angeles, CA: Audio Renaissance, 1998. 352 pp.

Davidson, Jeff. *The Complete Idiot's Guide to Managing Your Time.* New York: Macmillan, 1996. 220 pp.

Ellis, Albert. *How to Make Yourself Happy and Remarkably Less Disturbable.* San Louis Obispo, CA: Impact, 1999. 224 pp.

Ellis, Albert, and Melvin Powers. *A Guide to Rational Living.* North Hollywood, CA: Wilshire, 1998. 283 pp.

Frankl, Viktor E. *Man's Search for Meaning.* New York: Washington Square, 1998. 221 pp.

Goleman, Daniel P. *Emotional Intelligence.* New York: Bantam, 1997. 352 pp.

Lazarus, Arnold A., and Clifford N. Lazarus. *The 60-Second Shrink: 101 Strategies for Staying Sane in a Crazy World.* San Louis Obispo, CA: Impact, 1997. 176 pp.

Mayer, Jeffrey J. *Time Management for Dummies.* 2nd ed. Indianapolis, IN: IDG Books, 1999. 372 pp.

Schlosberg, Suzanne, and Liz Neporent. *Fitness for Dummies.* 2nd ed. Indianapolis, IN: IDG Books, 2000. 384 pp.

Seligman, Martin E. P. *Learned Optimism.* New York: Pocket Books, 1998. 319 pp.

Temes, Roberta. *The Complete Idiot's Guide to Hypnosis.* New York: Macmillan, 1999. 392 pp.

Index